Introduction to
Networks and
Telecommunications

Introduction to Networks and Telecommunications

Philip Avery Johnson
College of William and Mary

Writers Club Press
San Jose New York Lincoln Shanghai

Introduction to Networks and Telecommunications

Writers Club Press
an imprint of iUniverse.com, Inc.

For information address:
iUniverse.com, Inc.
5220 S 16th, Ste. 200
Lincoln, NE 68512
www.iuniverse.com

ISBN: 0-595-17670-4

Printed in the United States of America

To my wife, Margaret;
my children, Lori and Jeffrey;
and My granddaughter, Avery

Contents

Foreword

My motivation for writing what follows comes from teaching undergrad-uate and graduate business students over the past five years or so. I have come to realize and appreciate that business training requires a technical basis, particularly for those who continue into business where they become intimately involved with the technology of today. It is only when people get out into a career in or closely aligned with technology- based businesses that they look for answers that they have not been prepared to give. This is not the right time to look for these answers.

It is not the business students' fault: the computer science courses typi-cally deal with the idea that a computer is a monolithic device. When one looks for thoughts on how do computers talk to one another, you tend to fall back on ideas on how people talk—this is quite misleading to the problem at hand.

Even the business curricula, which leads one into discussions about the B-to-B and B-to-C new economy marketing and other issues, tend to avoid the way in which these industries work operationally. It is to this perceived gap that this book may aid.

My personal realization of the issues herein has not been an easy search; the first time I saw material on distributed issues with when Phil Bernstein of Harvard discussed distributed databases—Phil ended on the thought that this area was closed for further research because he had proved that further extensions were not doable. Then came work on standards, and about five years later I got into protocols, since I had been a software developer earlier in my career. Trying to put all the pieces together at one time would have been a lot better than doing it piecemeal. But, doing the piecemeal approach had the advantage of not being overwhelmed by the jargon, difficulty of the concepts and just the time it takes to let this information roll around in your mind, assimilate and become your own. So, I've taken a half-way approach—consider the really important concepts, but let the multitude of options of other researchers be better left to their texts. This book is meant as a true introduction, and I have taught it that way for the five or so years. This isn't the last word on this subject; but, if it generates interest for individuals to go further and investigate specifics elsewhere, the book has done its job.

January 2001

Williamsburg, Virginia

Acknowledgements

I owe a great debt to my mentors at Bell Laboratories: Mark Klerer and Jim Day: the knowledge about the OSI model, "layers", and network management.for networks. Thanks also go to Jerry Ash, my friend (and golf buddy), and Adolf Vogeley, my friend and funder over the years at Bell Labs.

I have been blessed with a number of people in academia who have been an inspiration: Ben Avi-Itzhak of Rutgers University (but also of Bell Labs, Bellcore, and the Technion); Larry Pulley and Gigi Kelley of the College of William and Mary.

Even in the standards work, domestic and international, I have rubbed shoulders with many great people. Sharing issues with them has given me a different perspective on what standards are, and why they are important. Specifically, Art Reilly of Bellcore, Marty Sullivan of Bellcore, Alvin Lai of ECSA and ANSI, Bob Beebe of Pacific Bell and Verilink, Bill Buckley of Verilink, Bill Cardarette of GTE and a host of others. Particularly in the development of SONET, I came quite close to Chuck Huffman and Everett Turvey of Rockwell—I recall our Thursdays in Northern California with great fondness—and nostalgia—at this distance. And the Europeans who got me to think more globally, wherever we happened to be.

Finally, to my family, Lori, Jeffrey and my wife, Margaret, who had to endure the trips to various standards meetings, but also to Margaret for putting up with blank looks when I have been working on this book, but should have been doing something around the house.

Thanks all.

Chapter 1—Introduction

Networks and telecommunications are typically discussed separately; this attempt is to discuss these subjects together in order to have an easier transition in developing future telecommunications services and products. A number of facets come together, each one of them being broken down in many ways first and then being integrated specifically in one way to define a particular application. But, we're getting ahead of the story.

1.1 The pieces of Networks

Data communications, distributed processing, protocol software and other issues have come together to define the technology underlying networks and telecommunications. Yet, an even earlier approach is extensively used: the separation of functionality to achieve very specific goals and the integration of specific pieces of this functionality to achieve a particular instance of networks. Even the way one looks at networks and telecommunications is understood by a particular instance of technology and where that instance sits in the spectrum of centralized/distributed functionality.

Typically, telecommunications sits at the centralized pole of functionality, as we will later see; networks, however, tend to favor the centralized approach. One example of networks, the Internet, has no structure, was not designed as a single monolithic structure, and has no centralized control or command—this being both its greatest strength and greatest weakness. Other networks tend to be a little more centralized in approach and implementation.

1.2 Network architecture

A natural way of integrating the different technology pieces or instances is to adopt a network architecture. A network architecture gives a perspective of how the different functionality can not only come together, but also provides a check to make sure that all needed functionality for communications exists.

Two ways of designing architecture exist: 1) the idea in protocol of defining different layers of functionality to specify the needed parts of communication, and 2) the identification of physical parts of a communication that require functionality for communication to proceed. In specifying either design, we come close to both realizations.

These various designs exist because of needs in the communication path. Typical functions requiring specification include:

1) Some basic activation of the communication path is required. This means that the communication path is enabled for communication use and that the identity of both sides of the communication paths is known and understood by all parties to the communication.

2) The enabled technology (also called a "source system ") that is transmitting a message must know that other enabled technology (also known as a "destination system") can receive a message.

3) Information transfer between the source and destination systems must be transparent to the communication path and the implementation of the transfer must be compatible to both source and sink systems.

From the logical (functional) viewpoint, this has led to the "three layer" model of communications. The "three layer" model uses the above needs or requirements and defines the three parts of a physical communication: 1) accessing the communication path, 2) the actual transporting of the information from site to site, and 3) the use within each end-system.

1.3 Business Communications

The overall use of a network is communications—the delivery of information from source(s) to destiination(s). In this book, unless otherwise stated, we will assume one system—to—one system communication. The extension to much larger networks, for the most part, is straightforward. However, what is this data that is being transferred from one place to another?

When engineers and scientists were the primary users of computers, the information of interest was primarily digital—numerical kinds of information. This categorization continued through the initial business users—accounting and finance, which was (and still is) interested in numerical results. As business use grew and expanded throughout corporate life, other kinds of data have developed in usage of computers: voice, digital (numerical) data, image and video data. Each one of these categories is necessary in today's environment; each also has very different needs in terms of resources. The following table illustrates data rate requirements.

Data Rates

Information type	Uncompressed data rate	Compressed data rate
Voice	64 kbps	8 kbps
Stereo Audio	88.2 kbps	12 kbps
Full Motion Video	45 Mbps	1 Mbps
Broadcast-quality NTSC Video	120 Mbps	3-6 Mbps
High-definition video, Broadcast quality	1500 Mbps	20-30 Mbps
Full-color still images, 400 X 400 pixels/in., 60 pages/min.	500 Mbps	45 Mbps

Source: [COX95] and [LYLE92]

Along with data rate, the response time of computing resources is a way of evaluating information and the effort it takes to generate it. Response time has a benefit-cost equation: the lower the response time (generally, a good thing), the greater the cost. Here, cost has two factors: 1) competing needs and 2) native computer processing power. Typically, response time is measured in two ways: 1) user response time, and 2) system response time. User response time can be defined as the time between the instant a user receives the last character of a message to the time of initiating the first character of the next message. System response time is the time between the instant the user enters the last character of a message to the first character of the response on the display device.

1.4 Standards and their impact

In order to maintain consistency between the various entities in the process of communicating with each other, it seems logical to make sure that all entities are communicating in the same computer language, where this computer language is specified in some standard fashion. In normal communication between humans, we will assume that one language is fine, but we typically aren't careful how we use this language—slang, colloquialisms, etc. We, as humans, filter and interpret the message-specific pieces (i.e., slang) without a second thought; this doesn't work for computers—the business of clearly specifying what pieces of a communication mean is the function of standards.

Standards proceeds in a number of different arenas: for computers, ANSI (American National Standards Institute) is the primary body in the United States; IEEE (International Electric and Electronic Engineering) Society and the ISO (International Standards Organization) are the main international bodies. For telecommunications, ANSI and its member, T1, are the primary U.S. bodies; the ITU (International Teletraffic Union) is the international body.

The purpose of standards is to unambiguously specify functionality and detail of communication so that it can be known by all participants of a communication, how one is to both send and receive information, and even how to initiate/terminate such communication. These above-mentioned bodies, in consensus fashion across their respective constituency, fashion agreed-to documents that comprise understanding of functionality.

What happens in a number of the succeeding chapters of this book actually was derived in one standards body or another, was then implemented by the many product manufacturers and placed into service by the body of service providers. This standards-setting process tends to occur in one of two ways: 1) a corporation which has great marketplace acceptance to its product/service can become the "standard-setter" in effect (thereby getting the rest of the industry to adopt the firm's product as the industry standard, and 2) standards are derived in an "open" process, where many materially-affected entities agree through consensus to a set of specifications. An example of the first instance is the AT&T Corporation before divestiture. At that time, AT&T was a regulated monopoly—in effect, the telephone company of the U.S. As such, it set the U.S. standards for telecommunications. More recently, it has been alleged that the Microsoft Corporation has controlled standards for operating systems and applications products, such as its OFFICE© product. In terms of standards for networks, the majority of the standards setting has been through the second alternative, that being the consensus-based, open process across many industries in that industry. In both case, standards, and particularly how the details of standards are put together, are exceptionally important to communication. We will deal with this phenomenon in a later chapter.

Chapter 2
—The Client-Server Impact

2.1 Background

It should not be surprising that the fundamental idea of computer design is incompatible with communication and networks. Originally, the computer was a single machine and the initial design derives from the Turing "finite-state machine". This machine was a piece of magnetic tape, being fed into a 'tape reader/writer with a control box attached. This control permitted the one character on the tape to be read, and would instruct the tape to be moved forward, back, or remain in position and would produce the next control instruction, for the next movement of the machine. This model of a computer has remained intact, primarily for theorecists. It wasn't long, in practical terms that the idea of getting data to and from the computer came about. The advent of printer, keyboard, mouse, and so on caused the above design to incorporate these I/O devices into what we think of as a computer. In fact, the addition of these different devices into one overall, integrated device caused the invention of the operating system to keep track and control these different devices and their interaction with the hardware. Actually, the operating system changed the computer from strictly a computing device into a network of various devices doing different functions, which require communications between not only the individual devices, but also the operating system.

The basic idea of processor-operating system-peripheral devices as a 'computer' has continued through various changes of processor technology, different operating system design, through the centralized main processor to the mini-processor and the desktop PC of today. However, the advent of the Internet and the World Wide Web (WWW), as well as many corporate and other networks) led to a change in philosophy of computer design in the early 1990s: client-server.

Client-Server (also known as manager-agent), or the client-server paradigm, has seen great growth since the early 1990s. Much of this growth has been supported by a number of industry segments: 1) applications- and database providers, 2) operating system vendors, and 3) workstation manufacturers. The applications- and database providers are in the business of offering business solutions to their customers; the client-server method offers expandability without complete retrofit and major expense. The operating system vendors were able to reuse tactical design for software in implementing client-server solutions; an example is the print spooling strategy, now incorporated into most operating systems, which closely resembles the Remote Processing Call of the client-server paradigm. The workstation manufacturers were looking for more performance and reliability in computer system design, offered by the client-server. Let's take a look at how client –server does all of this.

2.2 Definition of Client-Server

The client-server paradigm connects at least two computers across a network through a protocol of sending messages back and forth which define what kind of communication will be allowed at this instant. The "client" computer is that processor which is the source of messages for aid in processing its user's request; the "server" computer is that processor which responds through messaging to the "client" in a predetermined way, either by doing the complete job for the "client" or simply doing a portion of the processing or something in-between. The amount of work down-loaded from the client to the server is determined at the initiation of communication and can be categorized into the following:

5) *client-based processing* (also known as 'fat client')

6) *server-based processing* (also known as 'fat server')

7) *cooperative processing* (known as 'pier-to-pier'

Fat client represents processing done by the client machine; fat server is processing done by the server; pier-to-pier is a split between client and server- generally for performance optimization of the entire system.

2.3 Characteristics of Client/Server

Reasons for the development of this paradigm are many: the flexibility of the computing approach has allowed many industries to gradually grow from one computing environment into another, in a graceful (i.e., non-business-impacting) way. Thus, the end-user can remain quite comfortable using applications on the client-server machine environment, where changes can be imbedded on the server. This kind of flexibility has also given end-users great flexibility in upgrading to a faster environment: the user negotiations remain on the client with upgrades going to the server. This has also led to the idea of very small/inexpensive machines called "appliances", which tend to have very specific, yet limited, functionality; yet, this functionality allows for internet communications, which links the appliance to the server for processing.

This compartmentalizing of the computing resources is typically referred to as modularization. One additional aspect is that this allows for openness of applications to be performed.

Many businesses tend to think of this openness and modularity as a way to emphasize centralizing corporate databases, network management and other utilities, normally on the server. The implicit networking with the client means that support for these various functions can be centralized to one or a few places; this aids maintenance and ongoing operation of the system as a whole.

A categorization of pros and cons of this paradigm now follows.

Pros of client/server	Cons of client/server
Easy growth	Maintenance
Open systems	Retraining costs
Flexibility: multiple alternatives of functionality/cost operation	

2.4 The concept

The model of client-server came from the central ideas in operating system development: the concept of message passing between client and server; communicating who does what is directly analogous to the development of print spooling in general operating systems.

What is "spooling"? This concept allows a special software tool to initiate communication between operating system and the printer controller (generally, a part of the "printer") to cause the printer hardware to print a user-specified document. The key aspect is that the operation is transparent to the used—actually, the operation is activated by user-specific code, which enables the special operating system code to activate the printer hardware. A more detailed of the printer spooler operation now follows:

1) An application program performs an "I/O" instruction

2) The I/O instruction activates an operating system primitive command called a "trap". This is the only way that an application program can communicate with the operating system, other than a "call".

3) The "trap" collects various parameters about the I/O and puts them into a stack. Examples of the parameters are file name, number of copies, margin details, font, and color details. At times, these are added by the user through the user interface.

4) When the operating system scheduler allows it, the stack is sent to the printer controller.

5) When the printer controller detects that the printer is free, the stack is sent to the printer for execution.

6) At the end of execution, a message (usually, a parameter) is returned to the operating system. This message details successful execution or the reason for failure, if unsuccessful.

Two aspects of this detail are particularly of interest: 1) the execution of the printer is completely independent of the end-user (also known as end-user transparency), and 2) the actual mechanism of communication between operating system and printer controller (which was glossed over in the above). The idea of end-user transparency and a mechanism for communication are the basis for message passing.

2.5 Message Passing

In this section, we will first describe, in words, the process of message passing; we then draw a figure of this process. In both, we will retain the idea of end-user transparency and a mechanism (analogous to printer spooling) for communications.

The Process

We arrive at a point in an end-user applications program where we wish to do a piece of work. We will generally execute a "call" to transfer control to the operating system. As far as the end-user is concerned, program execution is still continuing in the currently running application program.

The interrupt handler of the operating system interprets the "call" instruction; information is gathered by the operating system to keep track on where to continue processing. This information comprises data, pointers to specific code and other parameters in the application code; this information is placed in a stack in the operating system.

1) Transfer of control within the operating system to the kernel (of the operating system) occurs. The sole function of the kernel is communication. The kernel determines the location (specifically, what machine is to perform the work), creates a message which encapsulates the stack, and sends the message containing the stack to the destination machine.

2) Once the destination machine receives the stack in its kernel, the stack is stripped from the message envelope, is forwarded to the interrupt handler, and is scheduled for execution. Upon execution, the results of the execution are placed in a stack in the destination machine's operating system and are returned to the kernel.

3) In the kernel, the results are placed in a message and are returned to the initiating machine. This message is received in the kernel of the requesting machine.

4) The kernel removes the stack and transfers the stack to the interrupt handler, which then schedules the application program to return to the place that it gave up control. The results are then returned to the application program for further direction of processing by the application program.

An illustration now follows:

Message Passing

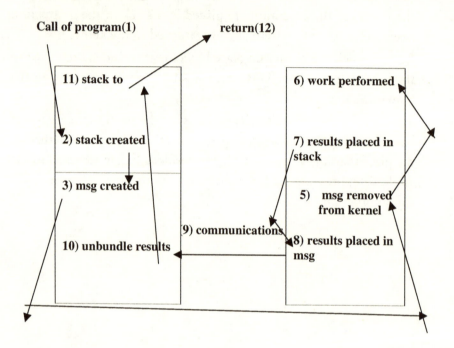

2.6 Remote Procedure Call (RPC)

The above procedure of using the operating system facilities to bundle necessary parameters, to construct messages for another system, and to transmit the message to another system, whether client or server, has the end-user transparency and communications properties discussed earlier. The above procedure is also directly analogous to the Remote Procedure Call of operating systems, as both use the same mechanism. We alternatively refer to the message-passing scheme for client-server as RPC.

In terms of the actual communication, a couple of things have been glossed over that should now be clarified. First, when the client is ready to send the message to the server, how does it know the name and/or location of the path/address in the network to use? The client-server paradigm uses a transparent mechanism (to the end-user) to specify the destination address. There are three mechanisms to accomplish this task, but only one practical one. The first, machine process addressing, uses the actual hardware address of the server for connection. In situations where there is only one server, this method is applicable, but it still requires one to know the actual hardware address, which limits practicality beyond one server. The second method, broadcasting a query to all potential servers on the communications link/network with the client, asks each server whether it has the functionality and the ability to process the client's request. If one such processor exists, it responds with its hardware address to the client; the kernel of the client's operating system appends this address to the message and sends the revised message as per the first method. This second method has the disadvantage of adding unneeded messages to not only the communication link/network, but also adds processing burden to all servers, including those which are not capable to do the client's work. The third method, implemented in virtually every environment today, is called the Domain Name Server (DNS). The DNS is an additional server appended to the communication network of the client. This server acts as a directory reference for the client, by retrieving machine addresses of servers able to do the client's work. The DNS acts much like the Directory Assistance of the phone system, where phone numbers are linked to people/firm information. The way in which DNS works is as follows:

1) The client sends a message to the DNS to find a server, which has the capability of doing the client's work

2) The DNS sends back a reply to the client with the machine address of a server that can perform the work

3) The kernel of the client appends the machine address to the message directed to the server for processing.

The second issue for the client is to decide whether to adopt a blocking or non-blocking primitive in its operating system. The difference is whether to buffer the message as it is being sent from the client that processing can continue at the client or to not buffer and hold processing until acknowledgement of message receipt at the server is received. In almost all cases, the non-blocking option is preferred.

2.7 Generic Client-Server Architecture

The various mechanisms acting in concert with the hardware and operating system platforms gives rise to a perspective of how to look at the client-server paradigm. One may view the various layers involved in processing client-server communication. Such layers of hardware/software is illustrated below:

Client-Server Architecture

Client	Server
Application logic	Application logic
Logic connecting application and system	Logic connecting application and system
Communication services(either communication software or operating system software)	Communications services(either Comm Software or operating system software)
Operating system	Operating system
Hardware platform	Hardware platform

2.8 Middleware

The phrase, "logic connecting application and system" requires some further explanation. What the transparency and other properties of the client-server paradigm do is they add software to either client or server. This software has the goal of providing or helping to provide a uniform means and access style to system resources across all platforms. In this sense, whatever version of application you decide to use (for example, MS Word 5 versus MS Word 6), the glue to make this work with your plat-form is the middleware. And, in this sense, the client-server mechanism is actually middleware—it allows the end-user to be connected transparently without being concerned how. Other examples of middleware occur: the database management systems allow the same transparency of system to user. Another example is an object-oriented implementation of the client-server paradigm.

2. 9 Summary

This chapter has dealt with the client-server paradigm: what it is, how it can be implemented, how it impacts processing in the underlying system. The kind of communicating between multiple systems is the basis for understanding how networks, or, for that matter, telecommunications work. What we will do is enhance our understanding of communications details from the overview picture we have so far.

Chapter 3
—Distributed Applications

3.1 Introduction

From the previous chapter of the client-server, it is clear that networking and telecommunications involve distribution of processing. What we consider here are some issues about distribution and distributed applications.

A number of issues are considered for distributed processing; benefits/disadvantages and organization. Organization tends to either vertical or horizontal partitioning. A categorization of some of the pluses and minuses follow:

Benefits	Disadvantages
Responsiveness	Test and failure diagnosis
Availability	Dependence on communication technology
Resource sharing	Equipment incompatibility
Controlled incremental growth	Network management and control
Distance and location independence	suboptimization

In summary, the added flexibility of the distributed organization outweighs the control and dependency issues that should be considered.

3.2 The applications

The fact that this paradigm has practical use has made it ever more useful in today's environment and tomorrow's. We now mention and explore a few of the applications.

The first major application of networking was *e-mail*, or electronic mail. Even though industries had thought that telephones were all that was needed, the versatility of e-mail offered users many unavailable features of phones. There were and are three primary components of electronic mail: 1) message preparation, 2) message sending, and 3) message receiving. The message sending process, independent of the end-user, uses the earlier methods of client-server for the actual transmittal of a message; both preparation and receiving have a number of commercially viable ways, usually involving specially created software for these functions. In fact, a standard involving the TCP/IP protocol, called the RPC 822, has been at the heart of many specific software packages enabling e-mail. For those desiring more detail, [STAL01] gives a good description; also, the RPC822 is directly available on the Internet.

The next major application, coming at about the same time of the PC revolution in the late 80s and early 90s, is Electronic Data Interchange (EDI). The advent of desktop machines, along with more centralized processors and large data inventories at many large corporations set the stage for methods to organize and operate on these data sources, as if the data were in one place. These methods allowed the centralized data base software for command and control to be expanded into the modern, distributed environment.

EDI has a number of benefits, the major ones being cost savings, speed, error reduction and security. These methods have also been important to create its own standard: X12 in ANSI. Clearly, the start-up cost, dissimilar or incompatible data or data platforms and incompatible database managers have been and continue to be issues for EDI.

These methods have also been used for *data warehousing*. Data Warehousing refers to the capture of both current and historical data into a single database structure. This concept is particularly adept for corporate mergers, where potentially incompatible database structures must be combined as economically as possible with a minimum of errors. The same idea has more recently led to enterprise systems, such as implementations of SAP and other products, where a single command database structure is implemented across a very large, disparate and distributed environment.

The last application discussed here, and potentially the most explosive in terms of ancillary applications, is the World Wide Web (WWW).

The history of the WWW is interesting. Developed by Tim Berners-Lee of the European Laboratory for Particle Physics Research (CERN) in the early 90s for specific purposes *within* CERN, it has become ubiquitous in worldwide computer usage. Berners-Lee had the objective of trying to get all the scientists, with differing language skills and from different countries, to cooperate, communicate among them and develop a single document for presentation to the European community. What Berners-Lee created was architecture to share information being created by these different scientists. This architecture, at its basis, allows for pages of information to be linked in a particular way in order to be accessed, retrieved and stored on the Internet. To accomplish this objective, Berners-Lee developed two new concepts: 1) a Web browser, and 2) a uniform resource locator (URL). These two concepts work with the idea of pages that are linked and can be located through these links. What the *browser* does is provide the access to the Web, typically through a web server, where the server maintains a database of information in the form of linked pages. These pages are then accessed; much like a database is accessed through its organization by the database management software, and retrieved as needed.

How we get to a particular page is the next step—and the second development of Berners-Lee makes this possible. Each page is identified by the URL. What occurs in the Web is that documents are treated as collections of pages, each of which has its own unique URL. Each page has a set of links (to other pages via their URL) to related pages on its server, and a set of links to other pages on other servers. Therefore, the process of retrieving information becomes a communication paradigm, using typical transactions (as seen in the client-server discussion) to do the access/retrieval functions. This might take the shape of the following picture on the next page.

The communication mechanism of the Web is a piece of software, typically set aside by itself, making use of the identical query-response transaction of the RPC message passing paradigm. As we will see, this standalone software embodies the TCP/IP protocol (Transaction Control Protocol/Internet Protocol) and a bit more. We will have more to say about this mechanism in the next-to-last chapter.

One last development that we have left until now is the language of the Web. Because of the concept that such a language must be invariant across many platforms, a single language, called HTML (HyperText Markup Language), was developed. The resulting HTML runs on many platforms, is simple in context, and easy to use. One feature is that similar structure of the language is used for text, images, data, whatever. HTML has great strength in its flexibility.

One should note that the recent developments in XML and SGML (both are extensions from HTML) have future promise for the Web; whether or not they will provide the increased functionality business desires in addition to HTML remains an issue for the future.

Web communications paradigm

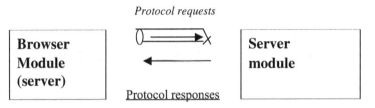

Protocol requests

Browser Module (server)

Server module

Protocol responses

Chapter 4
—Protocol Architecture

4.1 The Need for an architecture

One element of the communication process that has been under discussion is the fact that a data path exists between two (or more) points and that different things (or functions) occur along this path to create the total communications. We have assumed that the transfer of information goes along without any problem; we need to revisit this assumption and look specifically at each place of interface on this communications path and understand what is required for communications to work. To do this, we create an architecture in order to isolate different parts of the path in order to describe what must be done to assure smooth communications.

As we have mentioned before, different functions are performed at each of the stages to create communications. These different functions have generally been performed without care as to how they occur in a practical implementation: that is, they may be bundled into one large piece of software (such as the functions that comprise an operating system) or they may be partitioned into an arbitrary number of software pieces. In many cases, a natural partitioning occurs when we pay attention to the interfaces of the communications path. So, the architectural design intends to specify individual parts of the path, which gives guidance on how the functionality of the communications is partitioned. This specification gives rise to the *three layer model*, which is now described.

4.2 The three-layer model

From the client-server paradigm, we see that a message leaves the client operating system, goes across a communications path, and enters the server operating system. Thus, from the communications path viewpoint, we have an interface that needs further investigation: the network access/egress module (which we label 'access module'). This access module becomes the first layer. This layer deals with the functionality of exchanging information between a computer and the network (we shall now use this term for communications path) attached to the computer. For example, as we have seen with the client-server, we may need to access the name server (DNS) to obtain the destination address of a message. Further, because the type of network may be different (e.g., LAN, packet-switching, X.25), the services that can be performed across such network or communications path may also be different and may therefore require different software for implementation. So, the specifics of the interface are important, if not vital, to communications. And, it makes sense to separate the specific functions (and the software implementing such functions) into a separable unit. This implies that software in the other layers will work in whatever network is attached to the computer, since all the software for accessing the network is in one place.

Once the information is resident in the hardware, it is generally assumed that this information has been transferred in a reliable way form the sending computer to the receiving computer; to make this assumption a reality, we implement functionality ensuring reliable transfer into the system. As this functionality can be separated into a separable partition, we do this and call this partition the *transport layer*. This additional functionality becomes the 'second layer'.

Once we have received the information and have ensured that it has been received reliably, the computer is ready to perform actions on this information. This *application layer* contains the logic, which implement various user applications; an example is file transfer or e-mail

In summary, the *three-layer model* consists of software of separable functionality for communications. It is now time to start our consideration of the interfaces and different functionality available for construction of a network.

Chapter 5
—The Physical Layer

5.1 Introduction

So much for the protocol architecture of the last chapter. In order to actually transfer information from one place or point to another, some sort of signaling mechanism and a type of signal or signals are needed. The invention of flags identified troops, so that both friend and foe could know whom they were viewing. This mechanism came to be used on board ships, so that man-of-war of one nation could identify and be identified by other ships. Pirates even used a flag of sorts for identification purposes. Native Americans used smoke signals as a mechanism to communicate not only identification but also longer messages over long distances; so did other native populations in other areas. The nineteenth century saw electronic means beginning to displace the above visual means: telegraph being widely used in the United States to send messages back and forth. This medium used primarily a copper medium (although barbed wire and other electrical conductors were also used) which carried electrical signals, which conveyed a message (once translated), for humans. The dot-dash mechanism of the electrical signal became the basis for early radio and continues today for radio hobby enthusiasts.

5.2 Signals

The dot-dash of the telegraph illustrates the principle of the *Physical Layer.* The physical layer is the medium of transference of information on the network, via a predetermined signal. This signal has a number of properties that differentiate it from other alternative signals. The two most common signals for telecommunications are *continuous* and *discrete.* The continuous signal has the property of being totally connected from start to finish of the communication; the discrete has the property of having many start-stops in its pattern in communicating over time.

As signals in networks and telecommunications are primarily electromagnetic is nature; we can define the above continuous signal for networks as an **analog signal**—a continuously varying electromagnetic pulse that may be carried over an electromagnetic media. And, a **digital signal** can be thought of as a discontinuous electromagnetic pulse, such as a sequence of voltage pulses. This idea of pulses for digital signaling means that parameters involving time for this pulse (e.g., how often does a pulse occur, how one does it last on the media when it occurs, etc.) are vital for practical considerations, when we consider the transmitter-receiver pairs, connected by this signal. Such pairs are directly analogous to the client-server pairs of computers. We shall not concern ourselves about how the electronics of the transmitter actually constructs a signal through combinations of sine waves, having different frequencies. We shall assume that such waves can be created; now the issues of length of wave in time and amplitude of wave in volts are important for consideration. We close these thoughts with a few examples of both kinds of waves: voice signals, being continuous waves, exemplify analog signals, and TV waves, being streams of individual pulses of information detailing shading and color for precise screen placement.

5.3 Types of media

Networks and telecommunications are interested with digital information; we shall be interested in the physical media, which allow such signals to be carried by the medial itself.

A way of differentiating the kinds of media is to consider whether such media are *guided* or *unguided*. Guided media has the property that signals are sent across a solid medium, such as copper wire, fiber optics, or other. Unguided medial has the property of allowing electromagnetic signals to be carried, but not physically constrained, by the media itself. Microwave or radio are examples of unguided transmission.

Guided and unguided media have different characteristics of how signals are carried. These characteristics are bandwidth, transmission impairments/interference and distance between transmitter/receiver pairs. The *Bandwidth* of a medium can be defined as the difference between limiting frequencies of a continuous frequency band. For guided media, the types include twisted pair, coaxial cable, and optical fiber.

5.4 Guided media

Twisted Pair

A *twisted pair* is comprised of two insulated copper wires that are arranged in a twisted or wrapped fashion. This 'pair' of wires makes up a single communications link. In practical situations, many such pairs are combined in a sheath for economic reasons. The twisting is done to reduce the amount of electromagnetic interference ('crosstalk') between other pairs close by in the sheath.

It should be noted that twisted pair is the most common medium for both analog and digital signals in networks, at this writing. This medium is ubiquitous in almost all telephone networks and sees great usage elsewhere.

Coaxial Cable

Coaxial cable is comprised of two conductors; specifically, a wire conductor placed inside a hollow conductor with insulating material between the conductors. Typically, an insulating shield or sheath surrounds the hollow conductor. Compared to twisted pair, coaxial cable incurs much less interference due to its shielded nature. Thus, it can be used over longer distances and can support more transmitter/receiver pairs than twisted pair.

Cross-section of coaxial cable

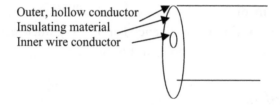

Outer, hollow conductor
Insulating material
Inner wire conductor

Coaxial cable enjoys wide use in a number of industrial applications, such as television distribution, local area networks in office environments and elsewhere for very short computer links (typically, 30 centimeters or less) and long distance telephone transmission.

Optical Fiber

Optical fiber, the newest of the three media discussed here, is a very flexible medium capable of conducting light. One typical example is very pure glass or silicon dioxide. Such media is comprised of a material, say glass, which has a cylinder-like shape and has three concentric pieces: 1) the innermost, called the *core,* 2) the middle layer, called the *cladding*, and

3) the outermost layer, called the *jacket*, which protects the fiber. The two glass layers have different indexes of refraction, and the cladding provides a mirror-like surface toward the core.

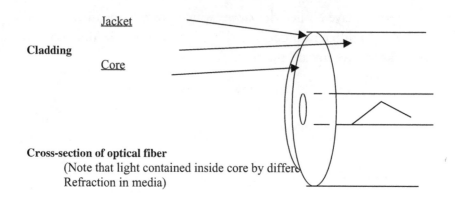

Cross-section of optical fiber
(Note that light contained inside core by differe
Refraction in media)

As with the coaxial cable, optical fiber has many industrial and military uses. The weight and size of this media, less than the twisted pair or coaxial cable, gives rise to its use in places which are cramped or difficult to access. Interference, a property of electromagnetic systems, is not applicable for fiber; this medium does not radiate much energy, which makes it better for applications where security is important. Even more transmitter/receiver pairs can be connected to this medium. These properties make optical fiber particularly useful in long-distance telephone transmission, local area networks, intracity trunks (or metropolitan trunks) and rural exchange trunks.

Optical fiber transmission operates as follows: light from a source enters the cylindrical fiber; rays from the light are not always carried by and through the fiber without colliding with the cladding; rays of light are thereby reflected at the cladding layer and are propagated along the fiber, assuming that these rays have a certain frequency; other rays (having different frequencies) are absorbed by the cladding layer. As the radius of the core is reduced, fewer and fewer frequencies will be reflected, until only one is carried—this is known as monomode or single mode transmission.

5.5 Unguided Media

Unguided media perform transmission through a medium such as air or water; reception of such transmission is performed through an antenna or other device that receives electromagnetic waves through this medium. These antennas can have different ways of how the waves are actually received. The media of most interest for the subject of this book are microwave frequencies; there are two major such frequencies: terrestrial microwave and satellite microwave.

Terrestrial Microwave

There are many antennas that look like small dishes or dish-like objects that make up terrestrial microwave. The major applications for such dishes are long-distance telecommunications transmission, for both television and voice-grade telecommunications. Some applications use this idea for site-to-site (say, buildings next to one another) links for closed—circuit TV or LAN applications.

Satellite Microwave

Such objects are actually relay stations of microwaves. They are comprised of two or more microwave transmitter/receiver pairs, which receives a microwave signal on one frequency, prepares the signal for retransmission and sends the signal on a different frequency. These frequency bands are known are **transponders** and the microwave transmitter/receiver pairs as **earth stations**.

A number of satellite microwave systems include television distribution, long-distance telephone transmission, and private business networks.

5.6 Guided versus Unguided: An example

Up until the early 1990s, the guided media was the dominant way of carrying signals. The advent of new technology has brought to bear a number of comparisons that are currently used by network designers for designing a new network: 1) price of different media, 2) services offered, and 3) intrinsic limitations of the technology. This has brought about a significant shift from satellite to optical fiber, as the technology of choice.

Comparison of Guided/Unguided media

Characteristics	Optical Fiber	Satellite
Interference	Not affected by electromagnetic waves	**Impact:** encryption needed for security
bandwidth	Order of gigahertz	Less than 100 megahertz
Multipoint	Only point-to-point	Easily implemented
Flexibility	Limited	easy

5.7 Interference

All communications systems can be impacted by interference; what interference does is change the signal that was sent from the transmitter in such a way that it is received in a different form by the receiver. Part of the design of the transmitter-receiver pair is to take action to minimize or eliminate such occurrences. Because of our consideration of digital signals, it is useful to look at interference, or impairments, to both the guided and unguided media.

Guided media

The major types of interference for guided media are noise, delay distortion, attenuation and attenuation loss.

Noise is created as a natural consequence of transmitting waves of energy and subsequently receiving them. What happens is that addition of extraneous energy occurs due to the environment: for example, heat occurs in all transmitter/receiver pairs. Such heat, in stirring up the electrons of the transmitted pulse of energy, can transform the pulse. Also, crosstalk and noise spikes such as lightening can add agitation to the signal.

Delay distortion occurs because signals at different frequencies travel at different velocities. Such signals are received in the receiver at different times for guided media (this phenomena does not occur in unguided media). This difference must be compensated for in the electronics; such compensation can only be partially done.

Attenuation occurs in the electronics of transmitter/receiver pairs, because amplifiers are used to boost the signal in places or reduce the energy level in other places. This action changes the energy, and thereby the form, of the signal itself.

Unguided media

For unguided media, as the signal propagates through the media (e.g., air), the signal disperses with distance. Consequently, the signal arriving at an antenna at the receiver has much less power than the originally transmitted signal. This factor makes unguided media susceptible to a number of factors that we now consider.

One of the main issues to be aware of is atmospheric absorption. Water vapor in the air is the main factor in atmospheric absorption. As such, it is a major factor in signal loss.

Multipath loss occurs when many physical obstacles occur in a signal's path that have the effect of creating many copies of the original signal that have varying delays. For example, skyscrapers and other structures in metropolitan areas can have this impact, particularly for point-to-point situations.

Other signal loss factors include refraction of radio waves, which can be impacted by weather and other natural phenomena, and noise resulting from heat generated from the transmitter/receiver pair.

5.8 The need for Repeaters

Because of the many ways by which a signal can be degraded for either guided or unguided media, consideration of the impact of this degradation on the receiver and on the ability of the receiver to correctly interpret the resulting signal is needed. What happens to the signal can be illustrated as follows:

Signal leaving the transmitter

As we see, pulses of energy, called 'square waves', are created by the electronics of the transmitter as it puts the signal on the media for transit. As the various impairments affect the signal over the distance of the transit, the resulting signal begins to look more like the following:

Signal arriving at the receiver

As in the figure, the signal is distorted and may not be recognizable. The receiver's design must accommodate this distortion by using sophisticated pattern recognition algorithms on the signal received and restoring the original character and pattern of the signal so that the signal can be sent further from the receiver to another receiver. This requires the receiver to correctly reestablish the intended pattern from interpretation of the algorithm. The process of applying pattern recognition to the signal, correctly interpreting and reestablishing the original signal and making it ready for further transmission on a bit by bit basis is the purpose of the *repeater*. Typically, the design of the electronics of the repeater is beyond the scope of this book. The repeater design can be that of a stand-alone device or built within both sides of the transmitter/receiver pair for implementation in the network. Such devices occur in the telephone networks in order to communicate over long distances. Some properties of repeaters are listed:

Spacing of repeaters in guided media

Media type	Distance in kilometers
Twisted pair	**2-3**
Coaxial cable	About 1; less once the rate exceeds a few Mbps
Optical fiber	A few kilometers for <100 Mbps (ex – about 15 for 1550 nm fiber)

5.9 Summary

The physical layer of data communications is vital for networks and telecommunications. Without an understanding of how and what are signals that are sent, it is impossible to determine how meaning should be given to a piece of signal at the receiver side. We have seen that there are both guided and unguided media, capable of carrying digital signals; various properties differentiate the media and are used by designers of networks to meet cost/benefit situations that different networks face. For this reason, one solution may not be best for a given network, even though it worked beautifully for another network. A designer will be interested in applying different solutions against the network to be considered, and arrive at a least cost or best benefit/cost solution. The following may aid in this search:

Type	Advantages	Disadvantages
Twisted pair	Inexpensive Easy to install	High frequencies a problem Limited bandwidth
Coaxial cable	Moderate cost Moderate bandwidth	Bulky Somewhat inflexible
Fiber optic	Much less interference Much larger bandwidth	Expensive to install
Satellite	No line-of-sight needed High bandwidth	High up-front cost Noticeable delays
Terrestrial	Same as satellite	Line-of-sight

We now turn to the problem of correctly interpreting signals, as we receive and interpret them at a receiver, in the next chapter.

Chapter 6
—Data Link Fundamentals

6.1 Introduction

The topic of this chapter is how to capture the signals in the form that they are sent over the network and convert them to something that a computer can understand. The next chapter will deal with how this can be done so that the expectation that what we send is what we receive is correct.

Even though we considered digital signals (also called square waves) in the previous chapter, the way in which the network carries such signals may be analog.

In such cases, we need to convert between digital to analog and back again. This aspect has given rise to modems (i.e., modulator/demodulator), that are pieces of hardware in the network that make these conversions. In fact, this function of converting signals also illustrates that the architecture is invariant between computer networks and communications networks. The following puts some terminology on this conversion:

Terminal   modem   circuit   modem   host computer

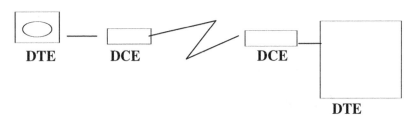

The idea of modems also gives rise to the DCE-DTE nomenclature; DTE equipment, such as computer laptop or mainframe, is defined as equipment that converts user information (or information in user terms) into data signals for transmission or converts received data signals into user information (DTE is Data Terminal Equipment).

DCE (Data Circuit-terminating Equipment) is the equipment that enables the conversion of signal between the DTE and the 'circuit' in the above figure. Today, modems provide additional functions from earlier modems that could either recognize a call or convert data, but not both. Newer, so-called "smart modems", work both in the establishment of a signal connection and also in the conversion of the signal, subsequent to the circuit establishment. We now consider the modulation of the signal on the network (or circuit).

6.2 Types of modulation

There are three methods of modulation that we discuss: amplitude modulation, frequency modulation, and phase modulation. All have use in various network situations.

Amplitude Modulation

In this type, binary ones and zeros are converted into sine waves, where the height (or amplitude) of the sine wave represents the binary value. Typically, the height would be high for a binary one, and low for a binary zero. The width of the sine wave does not change during the transmission. One issue that arises with amplitude modulation is that networks comprised of telephone circuits have the property that variations in transmission quality impact the amplitude greatly. This can cause the conversion process to misinterpret a zero for a one and vice versa.

Frequency Modulation

This type of modulation varies the frequency of the sine waves, keeping the amplitude of the signal constant. If signals in both directions on the media are needed, we need two frequencies (one for a binary one and the other for a binary zero) in each direction.

Phase Modulation

Phase modulation, also called phase shift keying, transmits data by changing the phase of the sine wave, carrying the signal. A sine wave normally repeats itself continuously, with one peak and valley followed by another peak and valley and so on. Shifting phase terminates the sine wave and restarts the wave a few degrees forward or backward. The main advantage of this technique is that only a single frequency sine wave is used to carry both binary ones and zeros in one direction; two frequencies were needed for the frequency modulation technique.

6.3 Encoding of digital data

Whereas modulation works for analog data (and is therefore a mainstay for the voice telephone network), different techniques are needed for digital data.

The motivation for digitally encoding analog signals comes from the advent of digital switching and data networks within the telephone system. The analog signals of the telephone network required conversion at the switches into digital information. The technique, called Pulse-Code Modulation (PCM), is a sampling methodology; the methodology considers the sine wave transmitted, considers the change in amplitude of the wave, takes the average of a sample, digitizes this average, and uses this digitized number for transmission. It should be noted that, although this process derives a digit for the amplitude, the actual transmission of the digit is in binary form. This PCM technique has proved very popular in telecommunications; the typical sample size is the length of the wave covering one-eight thousandth of a second. Eight thousand samples then comprise one second; one advantage of this procedure is that no difference in quality of voice on the voice network was noticed in numerous human factor studies. This one-eight thousandth of a second will arise again in the consideration of frames.

Digital encoding of digital data is needed where transmission across a digital network or digital subnetwork is required. The reason for this step, at first glance an unnecessary step, is the difficulty of dealing with long strings of zeros in data transmission. One might think that a positive amplitude (or negative amplitude) in voltage to send a binary one or no (or zero) amplitude in voltage to send a binary zero is all that is needed. This isn't the case. Intrinsically, electronic equipment configured into transmitter-receiver pairs, are different from any other such pair. Each pair has a clock (actually, each half of the pair has its own clock, which is not tied to the other clock of the pair). Thus, each part of the pair must determine time relative to other transmitter-receiver pairs, but also with respect to the other half of the pair in question. In computers, the mechanism enabling timing incorporates, typically, a crystal, not unlike the crystal enabling timing in many watches and other devices. And, crystals of the same material have the same inherent frequency of vibration. The difficulty arises in that impurities in the crystal produce very slight changes to the vibration frequencies—perhaps one vibration of difference in the 10th significant place of the vibration frequency. What this very slight difference does over many cycles is cause the clock in one-half of a transmitter –receiver pair to become noticeably different with respect to the clock in the other half of the pair. This puts an additional strain on the pattern recognition abilities in the receiver in recognizing the incoming signal (since the timing is off)—more misinterpretations will occur. This physical phenomenon is known as *jitter.* The following illustrates the inherent difficulties discussed:

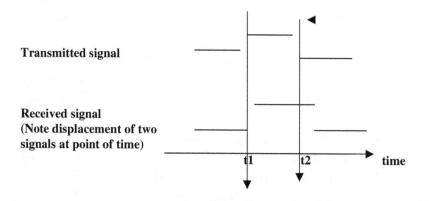

Transmitted signal

Received signal
(Note displacement of two
signals at point of time)

t1   t2   time

Ways to prevent this timing problem between transmitted and received signal have been explored for some time. What the current techniques designed to resolve the issue do is 1) transmit signals in such a way as to send timing along with the signal between transmitter and receiver so that the devices may recognize the inherent jitter, 2) resynchronize the clocks in both devices, and 3) keep transmitting, by taking into account the jitter in real-time. This is typically done by modifying the signal so that both transmitter and receiver can know precisely at exact start of a signal and the exact end of a signal. This can resolve the problem with long strings of zeros, which needs this resolution to continue the transmission. Methods to perform this action and to deal with error correction are the subject of the next chapter.

6.4 Digital encoding of digital data

There are a number of ways to transmit digital signals. Perhaps the easiest way (although not the currently implemented method in industry) is to use two different voltage levels for each of the two binary digits. Typically, a negative voltage is used for a binary one and a positive voltage for a binary zero. This method is known as *nonreturn-to-zero-level* (NRZ-L). An application is the very short connections between computer and another computer or modem (sometimes, such connections are within the hardware box—however, the idea of this connection is important, as we differentiate the computer and the modem.). A variant of NRZ-L is NRZI (NRZ, invert on ones). This scheme maintains a continuous voltage over a bit time (the time it takes to transmit a single bit). The data is translated to bits, depending on the absence/presence of a signal transition (i.e., the voltage switches polarity) at the start of the bit time. This is illustrated as follows:

Data	0	0	1	1	0
NRZ-L					
NRZI					

The second method, NRZI, is known as *differential encoding.* The name is given to those methods, which use the polarity at the start/stop boundaries of adjacent pieces of data to determine the encoding. These methods have a number of benefits over the more traditional nondifferential encoding techniques: 1) it is easier to determine change is polarity than change in amplitude, or absolute value in traditional signals, and 2) in practice, inversions of signal destroy traditional signals, but not polarity differential-based encoding. One disadvantage to such methods is the determination of where the signal actually starts/stops (jitter makes this more difficult).

Two additional encoding methods have been developed to counter this disadvantage. They are found in today's equipment implementations. These techniques use a *biphase* scheme—they have at least one transition per bit time and may have as many as two transitions. The advantages include: 1) synchronization is achieved, and 2) error detection can use the absence of an expected transition for information on errors. A disadvantage is the fact that greater bandwidth is required here than for non-biphase schemes.

The first such method, *Manchester code,* incorporates a transition at the middle of the bit time for each bit. This midbit transition becomes both the clocking mechanism and the data: a high to low transition represents a one, and a low to high transition represents a zero. This code is implemented in the Internet.

The second method, *Differential Manchester code*, incorporates midbit transitions only for clocking purposes: zeros are denoted by the presence of a transition at the start of a bit time, and a one by the absence of such transition. This method is implemented on token-ring LANs in industry. (Note that differential Manchester assumes that no transition has occurred at the time before the first zero for a low-high pattern.)

Chapter 7—Timing and Errors

7.1 Timing and timing strategies

From the previous chapter, we have seen how the problem of long strings of zeros arises as a timing issue. For example, say we wish to transmit 1000 bits from one computer to another. Assuming that they are transmitted at 10,000 bits per second (bps), each bit would be transmitted every .01 ms., as measured by the receiver's clock. If the receiver measures pulses at the middle of the pulse wave, the sampling would be every .01 ms. If the jitter of the clocks corresponds to a drift of the clocks of 10%, the first sampling would be .1% of a bit time away from center. Practical indications are that strings of about 100 zeros (800 bit times) are sufficient to introduce misrepresentations into the received string. So, how do we deal with the issue of resynchronizing the clocks?

7.2 Asynchronous Transmission

Two strategies have evolved to perform the desired synchronization. The first is called *asynchronous transmission*. The way of dealing with the problem, according to this strategy, is to **not** send long strings of zeros, or bits. In this strategy, information will be sent one character at a time, where a character can be between 5 and 8 bits in length. Timing then only has to be maintained for the one character; over one character, the slip or drift of the clocks due to jitter is not statistically significant; thus, the drift is not a problem, as the clocks can resynchronize at the start of the next character.

Each character has a specific pattern and method of starting/stopping the transmission. Typically, when no transmission is ongoing, a continuous string of binary ones is transmitted (for timing purposes, thereby maintaining the continuity of the link). This can also be thought of as an idle state, realized by this continuous string of binary ones. When information is being passed, the signal for the beginning of a character is a binary zero, also called a *start bit*. This bit is followed by between 5 and 8 bits that make up the character, which itself is followed by a *parity bit*. The parity bit is used as a check on whether an error has been introduced in the transmission. A convention between transmitter and receiver is constructed: if the number of bits in the character (the 5 to 8 bits of information) is even, the parity would be zero and the parity bit would be set to binary zero; if odd, the parity would be one and the parity bit would be set to binary one. This process would repeat itself for the construction of the next character, and so on.

7.3 Synchronous Transmission

The second method of achieving timing synchronization with the transmitter-receiver pairs is *synchronous transmission*. With this method, bits are transmitted in a continuous fashion, but *without start and stop codes.* Bits tend to be organized in bunches, known as *blocks,* which can be many characters long. For this organization, two ways exist to achieve synchronization: 1) provides a separate clock interface between transmitter and receiver, and 2) embed clocking information in the data signal itself. Although providing a separate clock interface is workable over short distances, it suffers the same problems identified for longer distances. Also, the cost of this separate hardware/software solution makes this alternative prohibitive. We consider the embedding Manchester.

An additional synchronization is required for synchronous transmission; as data is being expressed as blocks for this case, a way is needed to distinguish the end of one block and the start of the next block in sequence. Beginning each block with a preamble bit pattern, and ending each block with a postamble bit pattern does this. Also, additional data providing control for the data link procedures in this particular network is added. Summing up, each block is comprised of a preamble, postamble, control information, and user information or data. We also call this block as *frame.* The exact layout of bits depends on the specific data link procedure being used for the network being considered.

For applications involving low-speed terminals or computers, asynchronous transmission is the most common implementation. However, where large to moderate data transfer needs or intensive communications requirements exist, synchronous transmission is the method of choice. This arises from the inherent efficiency of synchronous techniques: fewer bits are needed for control and synchronization than for asynchronous. A typical asynchronous situation has more than 20% overhead because of the one-character view; synchronous overhead may be less than 1%.

The first frame in use was the high-level data link control frame (HDLC), which arose in the 1970s. Subsequent frame structures have modeled themselves on the HDLC architecture. The operation of this frame (and others like it) is straightforward: exchange of both user data and control information in a specific format within the frame itself. The specific fields comprise an HDLC frame:

Flag: used for synchronizing start/stops of a frame. A typical flag for this purpose is the pattern 011111110.

Address: the physical designation of the receiver within the network; this field is usually 8 bits long, but can be extended. In Internet applications, this field may be 128 bits long.

Control: identifies the functions and purpose(s) of the frame

Information: comprised of user data; this field has variable length

Frame Check Sequence (FCS): error detection purposes

False flags and "stuffing/destuffing"

Recalling that the flag was assumed to be a specific bit pattern, 01111110, it is possible that a portion of the data has the same pattern; this would then be recognized as a flag, by the receiver. This pattern is then a 'false flag', as it is interpreted as a flag, but is not such. To avoid the problem of false flags, stuffing/destuffing was invented. Once a pattern has been designated as a flag, the computer then, prior to adding the flag to the frame, will stuff a zero bit between the fifth and sixth one of the above pattern, making the 01111110 in the data become 011111010. The flag is then added and the frame is transmitted. At the receiver side, the flags are stripped out (as there are no false flags); then, the data is destuffed—the zero bit between the fifth and sixth one is removed, returning the data to its original state. This process is always done, for the reason mentioned.

Typical HDLC frame format

Flag	Address	Control	Information	FCS

Now that the frame format has been detailed, we see that other parts of this format need a bit more explanation: 1) the control field, and 2) the frame sequence check.

Control fields are intended to contain information to control the frame in a number of different ways. There are three types of control information: 1) information, 2) supervisory information, and 3) unnumbered information. The I-frame contains 1) a send sequence number, a receive sequence number, and some poll/final bit information. This helps to keep/reestablish the correct sequence of frames, if, for some reason, they have become unsequenced. The S-frame contains 1) supervisory function bits (which designate what functions are to be performed by the information sent in this frame) and 2) a receive sequence number. The U-frame contains the unnumbered function bits, which have a similar purpose to the S frame.

Although the information field and the address field have clear purpose, the same cannot be said about the control field. It is noted that the first one or two bits identify the *type* of control field in the HDLC frame. The following table lists some of the functions being transmitted:

HDLC commands and meanings

Name of command	Description of operation
Information (I)	Exchange user data
Supervisory(S)	
- Receive Ready(RR)	Positive acknowledgement
- Receive Not Ready(RNR)	Negative acknowledgement
-reject (REJ)	Negative acknowledgement – go back
Unnumbered (U)	
5) set normal response/extended mode (SNRM/SNRME)	Set mode
- set asynchronous response/extended mode (SARM/SARME)	Set mode
- set asynchronous balanced extended mode	Set mode
set initialization mode (SIM)	Initialize data link level control functions In addressed mode
Disconnect (DISC)	Terminate logical connection
Request disconnect	Request for DISC command
Request initialization mode	Request for SIM command
Reset (RSET)	Resets send,receive sequence number
Test (TEST)	Exchange information
Frame reject (FRMR)	Reports receipt of bad frame

The HDLC operation is comprised of three pieces: 1) initialization of the link in order to exchange frames in a meaningful way, 2) data exchange, and 3) termination of the link connect. Concerning initialization, this function commences once either side of the connection issues one of the set mode commands. Set commands perform: 1) signals the other side of the connection that initialization is requested, 2) specifies the mode, which concerns control of exchange, and 3) specifies whether 3- or 7-bit sequence numbers are to be used.

Data transfer occurs after a logical connection is established. The I-frames are exchanged: the send and receive sequence numbers deal with flow and error control. Concerning the disconnect stage, either side of the connection can initiate a disconnect. Once received by the non-initializing party, the link is terminated.

7.4 Error Detection by the Cyclic Redundancy Check (CRC)

You may recall that the Frame Check Sequence (FCS) field of the HDLC frame was left for discussion. The FCS field was used for error detection. More recently, due to updated algorithms and better hardware capabilities, this function is now called the CRC and uses the space in the HDLC frame that the FCS previously occupied. In the process of forming a frame for transmission, specifically the CRC portion, a calculation is made on the bits so far comprising the frame. The results of this calculation are then inserted into the frame as the FCS field and the frame is ready for transmission. Upon being received by the receiver, the identical calculation is performed on the bits received, and the result is compared to the value stored in the incoming frame. Typically, this results in a binary value with two outcomes: yes, values compare, and no, the values don't compare. If the values don't compare, the receiver assumes that the data has been corrupted during transmission and requests the transmitter to resend the frame. The following illustrates this:

Sender	Receiver
1. Prepares message	1. Receives message and CRC
2. Calculates and adds CRC	2. Calculates CRC
3. Sends message with CRC, comprising complete HDLC frame	3. Compares received CRC with computed CRC; if bad, retransmit frame

This method is powerful in that it finds errors is in the order of 2 to the minus Nth, where N is the length of the CRC in bits. Typically, modern computers of the current time frame use CRCs of either 32 or 64 bits in length. An example of a CRC computation follows>

We assume that the frame data to transmit is 110011, and that the algorithm will be to divide the frame data by the polynomial x to the third power + 1, or 1001, using one's complement arithmetic. For a Nth order polynomial, we add N+1 zeros to the frame data for the computation:

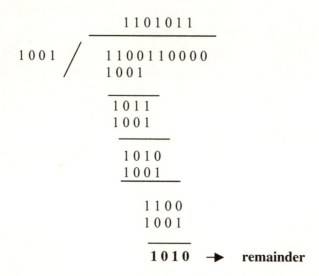

The transmitter transmits the remainder as the FCS (now, CRC) field of the HDLC frame. For the receiver side, if we repeat the one's complement division on what is sent, i.e., 110011101 divided by 1001, we see that the remainder is zero. For this algorithm, zero is interpreted as error-free; a non-zero result means a problem has occurred in the string (i.e., the transmission of the string) and the string is to be resent. So, in this case, we have successfully sent a frame that is error-free. Typically, this process is incorporated in hardware for performance reasons.

Chapter 8
—Multiplexing and Compression

8.1 Introduction

Once the basic network idea of transmitting between one point and another is realized, the mission of network design is to then make this transmission as efficient as possible—perhaps a better term is as cost-effective as possible. This motivation to be more cost-effective has led to more complicated network mechanisms that will be discussed over the next few chapters. However, in data communications, it is a given that the higher the data rate, the more cost-effective the transmission facility; it is also a given that most data communications devices require modest or relatively modest support. These givens have led designers to see if there is a way to pack as much data as possible into each and every link so that the package is the best in cost-effective measures. This has led to two techniques: multiplexing and compression.

8.2 Multiplexing

Multiplexing is a process which blends several information sources that require transmission from one point to another and have a given transmission capacity, thereby sharing a communication facility. This idea is shown in the following:

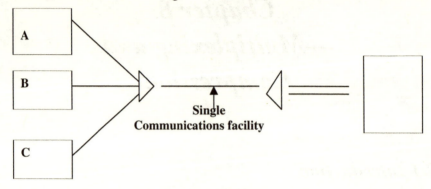

8.3 Frequency-Division Multiplexing

Frequency-division multiplexing (FDM) is a widespread application of a form of multiplexing. Cable TV is a big application, where many signals comprising multiple TV channels are carried on a single communications medium, the coaxial cable. What happens in FDM is that each channel to be carried is modulated onto a different carrier frequency and that sufficient separation of the various signals exists such that the bandwidth of the signals does not overlap. The separation assumes that each signal has a specific bandwidth, centered on its carrier frequency (i.e., channel), then adds some additional bandwidth to prevent interference; these added areas of bandwidth are unused for transmission of user signals.

For example, consider the transmission of three signals simultaneously over one facility. We assume that the bandwidth of such signals is 6 MHz, with effective bandwidth between 1 and 5 MHz. Using amplitude modulation on a 84 MHz carrier, the first signal in question becomes raised to a bandwidth of 58 to 64 MHz; in the same way, the other two signals can be raised to 64MHz to 70 MHz and 70 MHz to 76 MHz, respectively. Once received, this 58 to 76 MHz signal can be separated into three frequency bands, and then by demodulating each of the three, we arrive back at the three original signals.

The frequency-division multiplexing technique has other applications in the telecommunications arena. The telecommunications networks, dealing with long-distance signals and short-haul signals, have used the technique extensively, particularly for voice-grade communication. Interestingly, this technique is more efficient than digital alternatives in terms of bandwidth. However, the fact that both the noise as well as the user signal is amplified and the recent enhanced cost-benefits for digital hardware has led to a different multiplexing method, described in the next section.

However, the cable TV application is quite prominent at this writing. The analog TV signal fits well within a 6 MHz signal; the black-and-white video is amplitude-modulated onto a carrier signal with about a 5 MHz bandwidth. Separate color subcarrier and audio portions are encoded onto a 6 MHz signal with the black-and-white. As coaxial cable can have up to 500 MHz bandwidth, many channels of TV can be carried. The following table lists some of the frequency allocations for cable TV in the U.S.:

CATV frequencies (partial)

Channel identification   Band (in MHz)

Channel identification	Band (in MHz)
2	54-60
3	60-66
4	66-72
5	76-82
6	82-88
7	174-180
8	180-186
9	186-192
10	192-198
11	198-204
12	204-210
13	210-216
FM band	88-108
14	120-126
15-22	6MHz bands from 126 to 174 MHz
23-53	6MHz bands from 216 to 402 MHz
54-61	6MHz bands from 72-120MHz, with certain bands, already taken for Ch5,6 and FM

8.4 Synchronous Time-Division Multiplexing

The first of two time-division multiplexing (TDM) methods, called synchronous TDM, is workable when the data rate of the physical medium exceeds the required data rate of the signals that are to be transmitted on the medium. Interleaving parts of each transmitted signal simultaneously with the other signals in time does this. The idea is illustrated as follows:

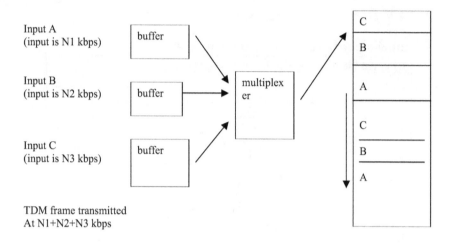

The above example has three channels, each of which is transmitting to a buffer, where the data is briefly buffered. Typically, each buffer is one character (or one frame) in length. The buffers are viewed in round-robin fashion, and a character (or frame) is extracted from each buffer to enter the multiplexer. It is implicitly assumed that these buffers are emptied before more data can be downloaded. These data are then placed into a superframe, with a character (or frame) from the first input source, then a character (or frame) from the second input source, and so on. The data rate of the multiplexer must be at least the same as the sum of the three input sources. This arrangement of characters in time, sequenced as it was across the characters of the input sources, can be synchronous or asynchronous and is transmitted either digitally or in analog. The reverse process is done when it is desired to split up the composite signal into the individual data streams: it is called *demultiplexing*.

The formation of the source characters into a composite frame along with a character/bit pattern denoting timing is what gives the synchronous property to TDM. Typically, we have the following illustration:

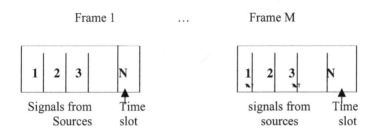

The information in a particular time slot for one source, say N, connected with the information in the analogous time slot in the next frame is called a *channel*. The slot length equals the transmission buffer length for either asynchronous or synchronous sources. Typically, the process of connecting channels bit interleaving for synchronous sources.

8.5 Compression

Compression is about removing redundant elements from data prior to the time that such data are sent across a network. This works for all kinds of data: text, image, and video. Clearly, after transmission, this method must be done in reverse to the data in order for the receiver to have the same data that the transmitter started with. This is known as *decompression*.

In essence, compression replaces the redundant elements in data by a code or symbol, so that the receiver can translate the compressed data back to its original form. Many such codes for compression are in use in networks. Some, known as loss *compression techniques,* allow for recovery of the exact original data at the receiver.

Video compression has become ubiquitous on desktop and laptop computers and the Internet-World Wide Web applications. Because of the vast amount of data typically associated with video, it may not be evident that this type of data has a high amount of redundancy, and is easily compressed.

Although three compression methods are in vogue today, much activity continues on exploring additional cost-beneficial alte4rnatives. The methods currently standardized are 1) M-JPEG, 2) MPEG and 3) ITU-T H.261. Because all of the current methods of video compression result in approximations of the original data when decompressed, they are all called *lossy* algorithms. It is beyond the scope of the book to deal with these algorithms in detail; however, the general method for all the current algorithms can be described as or approximated by the following seven-step process:

1) preliminary scaling and color conversion
2) color subsampling
3) discrete cosine transformation
4) quantization
5) run-length encoding
6) Huffman coding
7) Inter-frame compression.

Chapter 9—
Telecommunications
Background

9.1 Introduction

Considering that the aspects of data communication have dealt with invention of new or novel techniques and then inventing more efficient ways of doing the same thing, we turn our attention to telecommunications. Many of the data communications aspects that we may have attributed only to data communications are the backbone of modern telecommunications. In fact, the premise of this effort is that the two—telecommunications and data communications—are interrelated in inseparable ways. At this juncture, it may make sense to relate some of the historical background so that further work of data communications can be seen as an application within telecommunications.

9.2 Early Background

Bell's most famous invention, the telephone, kin 1876 was not the prime interest of its inventor. In fact, the telephone had come out of Bell's desire to help the deaf; it wasn't long, however, before this instrument became a needed device of business. Bell, as well as others, formed various companies in the United States to offer telephone service. At first, telephones were really implemented on a point-to-point basis: that is, as one person/firm wanted to communicate with another person/firm, facilities would be installed between the pair and service would begin. As demand grew, the concept of a telephone number was invented in 1879. This led to the idea of a *cordboard*, where cords—telephone connectors—could connect the various parties from one port of the cordboard to another port, where all the cabling would now come into the cordboard and have specific terminations. The alternative was to have 20 phones or so for each customer/business person, which was soon becoming unwieldy in the field. Western Electric, the manufacturing firm, was purchased by Bell in 1881. The demand kept growing at an ever-increasing rate. Even the load on the cordboards, congestion was becoming a problem. In 1891, the first switch (called the *step-by-step)* was invented and deployed, in order to automate the cordboard function of connecting the calling customer with the called subscriber. As the size of the business increased, Bell's firm found that it needed to combine and consolidate with other firms; the result, AT&T, was formed in 1900. Quite quickly, the firm established itself as a vertically integrated firm, with Western Electric (manufacturer) and Bell's original service establishment as the service provider. In 1910, the Department of Justice sued AT&T under the Clayton Act for monopolistic practices; the Kingsbury Agreement of 1911 started the idea of a regulated monopoly, with the provision of providing service to customers, even if it might not prove profitable to AT&T, as a public good.

9.3 Middle happenings

As the number and impact of inventions for the AT&T firm started to grow, the firm decided to establish the Bell Laboratories in 1925, primarily to deal with the research in coming up with ideas for the manufacturing of phone equipment. The commercialization of radio in the 1920s gradually began to have impact. Most early radio stations operated at perhaps one to five watts of power. Their range was limited to maybe a portion of a town or possibly to a few square miles. As advances in receivers and transmitters allowed increased power to transmit and receive signals over much greater distances, competition and conflict started to occur between radio stations, even those widely separated, when signals from the stations started to interact, causing neither signal to be heard. This led to complaints of listeners, first to the stations involved. When action from the stations wasn't enough, complaints were made to state and, finally, the federal government. The idea, that a governmental agency should provide a public service to allocate radio spectrum to potential stations, gained ground. The idea that, such an agency could also monitor and control other forms of telecommunications, also gained ground. In 1934, the Federal Communications Act was passed. This law was designated to deal with some of the complaints coming from radio, but also would be broad enough to impact the telephone industry. To do this, the 1934 Act created a federal agency, the Federal Communications Commission (FCC), to be the public's monitor and control wing of the federal government. As the World War II led to unprecedented inventions—radar being one—the environment of new technology changed dramatically. In 1947, three Bell Labs researchers invented the transistor. This invention, at the time, was seen by a number of individuals in telecommunications to be earth shaking, as it ultimately came to be seen by all. In fact, the AT&T management wanted to use this invention as the key piece of their plan for getting into computers, which were just starting to emerge. IBM was still dealing with electromagnetic adding machines at the time, and had a very hazy vision of how computers would impact their industry. In 1949, the advent of computerization was starting to take shape and AT&T wanted to use its invention to reinvent its corporate self.

At this point, the Department of Justice brought suit against AT&T under monopolistic violations of the FCC constraints; the real reason was the patent for the transistor that AT&T held was foreseen as the enabler for not only the computer industry but also the consumer electronic industry. In 1956, the Department of Justice and AT&T agreed on the 1956 Consent Decree. The major portions of this act, besides the reassertion of power and jurisdiction of the FCC, were two: 1) to require AT&T to license various patents from Bell Laboratories to requesting organizations at a very low price (definitely not anything that a particular patent was worth in the open market), and 2) to require that AT&T not enter the nascent computer industry. As IBM and others began their run toward computer power in the late 1950s and 1960s, AT&T executives grumbled about what might have been.

9.5 End Game

As the computer industry came to fruition, some unintended consequences started to appear on the telecommunications scene. First was the desire of a number of the computer giants of the 1960s to have their own private networks; next was the open question of having access to AT&T facilities through non-Western Electric equipment. Technology also was a player, as the radio and microwave inventions during World War II helped a fledgling company doing dispatching of trucks between St. Louis and Chicago to change its earlier technology to microwave: MCI (Microwave Communications Inc.). As MCI began to expand, and lobby the FCC for more access, the control of facilities and who can use them heated up. In 1968, after many debates within the industry and in the courts, the Carterphone decision was upheld. This decision dealt with whether a non-Western Electric device could be attached to AT&T's network. In the decision, the FCC mandated that the monopolistic control of AT&T over network access was no longer permitted. Not too long after this decision, the Department of Justice again brought suit against AT&T, starting in 1974, for violation of the Clayton Act. This action, after much additional debate, brought about the Modified Final Judgment (MFJ) that was agreed to in 1983 and implemented 1984. This judgment separated the local exchange service companies of AT&T from the long distance service part, the Bell Laboratories and Western Electric. This break-up of the vertically integrated AT&T was clearly one of the most controversial decisions in the long history of telecommunications. Because of the technology needs of the local companies (now called the Regional Bell Operating Companies (RBOCs)), a new entity, Bellcore (now, Telecordia) was formed to be the research arm of the RBOCs. However, AT&T, rather the newly reconstituted AT&T, was allowed to compete in the computer industry. The original intent of the MFJ of the federal government was to focus segments of the business on specific aspects of telecommunications. This thought motivated various companies to increase their vertical integration in order to expand revenue opportunities almost from the start.

One side activity that quickly came about was the domestic telecommunications process. Up to the point of divestiture (another name for the MFJ), there was one domestic player in telecommunications—AT&T. Internationally, the State Department, due to its treaty responsibilities, was the U.S. member in telecommunications debates. Typically, AT&T supported the representative of State with experts in various technical areas. This all changed at divestiture. A process was created, setting up the domestic telecommunications body and the way in which the Department of State would carry the will of the U.S. to the international standards body, the ITU. This process allowed for consensus of all materially affected corporations and other entities to be established for agreement for a standards position in an aspect of telecommunications. This is discussed in a later chapter, particularly the impact of this process, and its importance, on the networking and telecommunications industry.

9.6 The Telecommunications Act of 1996

Almost from the outset, divestiture was under substantial pressure from the pieces of AT&T to change. The local companies thought that they should have more freedom to manufacture equipment; at divestiture, they were almost required to buy from a competitor—AT&T. The long distance company wanted to play in the local carrier's area. New technology such as fiber optics and wireless phones opened up unforeseen alternatives that everyone wanted to manufacture/use. The federal government was under pressure to settle increasing numbers of court suits, partially brought about by loopholes in the divestiture agreement. Even within the local community of RBOCs, tactics such as goodwill and playing together was disbanded early on, when various RBOCs decided to compete (Yellow Pages is an example) in other RBOC's territory.

It had become clear by the 1990s that something had to be done: not only was technology driving new products, but increasing demand for newer and faster services were desired. Local competition needed a uniform policy; carriers of various stripes wanted to compete in broader areas, and, even the federal government wanted to implement a list of desires for its constituents. The stage was set for a revision in the divestiture agreement to be created.

The Telecommunications Act of 1996 was the result. One interesting aspect of the Act is that it removes the ability of a state to approve competition in local communications within its territory. Other features are that the Act redefines the relationships between the FCC and the state regulatory agencies in that the states determine the cost basis for competition only.

The major portions of the Act are:

1) resources (previously domain of the RBOCs) can be made available to Competitive carriers for the following:
   a) number portability
   b) dialing parity
   c) access to rights-of-way, including poles
   d) reciprocal compensation

e) unbundled access

f) co-location ;

in addition, a timetable must be provided to a requesting carrier when it requests

interconnection. Deadlines for providing such timetables are specified. The parties agree costs for such interconnections to, with the local Commissions also concurring.

2) Prohibitions of barriers to market entry are provided in the Act

3) Universal Service must be provided and be affordable

4) "Slamming", the process of submitting or changing a subscriber's telephone local provider without authorization by the subscriber is prohibited

5) RBOCs are allowed entry into the long distance (formerly known as the inter-LATA area) arena. The local carriers must satisfy a "14-point checklist", ensuring that the RBOC requesting long distance entry has also provided for local competition to its long distance competitors.

6) RBOCs may manufacture once they have entered into the inter-LATA market

7) Electronic publishing is allowed through a separate subsidiary of a RBOC.

In addition, the Act also deals with cable service. Some of these provisions include:

8) cable rates are deregulated once effective competition in the area exists.

9) Allocation of spectrum issues are left to the FCC

10) RBOCs are allowed to offer video programming

11) Regulations on obscenity and pornography were passed, but later found to be unconstitutional

12) The interconnection and resale rules do not apply to the rural telephone companies (less than 50,000 access lines)

Without question, the Act is quite large in scope: it is also quite arcane, because of the complex issues of interconnection, the legal complexities inherent in the wording, and questions of technical resources at the local level. What has happened since the Act was passed has been a continuation of legal action and regulatory maneuvering. Also, a number of the RBOCs have consolidated, creating (at this writing) two or three RBOCs; this has led to major downsizings of middle-level staff managers at all the companies, local and long distance. In addition to the consolidations, a number of initiatives with international partners have also taken place. Wireless has created a number of new corporations and subsidiaries of existing corporations. The cable industry has combined and is ready to compete in the telephone arena (for example, cable modems at very high speeds, relative to the telephone offerings). Vast changes to a business/businesses with technology as a leading factor and leading reason for change.

Chapter 10
—The Telecommunications Switch

10.1 Background

From its earliest days, the telecommunications system has had the problem of how to concentrate calls from one subscriber to another on fewer and fewer facilities. At the start, phones were installed such that this instrument was connected to one and only one party; in some executive suites of the 180s and 1890s, lthere may have been twenty or more individual phone sets on the executive's desk. This led to interesting times when one phone was ringing and had to be answered. This physical connection was made a little more logical when "cordboards" were invented. Cordboards were constructed with two sides to them: one side, called the "incoming trunks", was connected to the phones which could possibly make a call; the other side, called the "outgoing trunk" side, was also connected to the subscriber base. When a call arrived at the cordboard, it appeared at the given port on the incoming trunk side that corresponded to the calling party. The incoming call, at its arrival at the cordboard, also signaled an operator. An operator responded, found out who the calling party wanted to be connected to, and then connected the incoming call port to the port on the outgoing side that denoted the physical appearance of the "called" party, who the originator wished to talk to. What this did is greatly simplified the twenty phone sets on desks to a single instrument; this simplification was traded off for the cordboard and its operation and maintenance. Over time (concurrent with growth in the number and length of calls being placed), this cordboard became burdensome and another method was looked for.

10.2 The early switch

About 1911, the first electromagnetic switch was invented, installed and used in the telephone network. The idea came from the cords connecting the incoming and outgoing sides of the cordboard. The thought was to replace the human labor was a mechanism doing the same function. This, as an aside, led to the invention of the dial tone (in order for the calling party to send a signal to the telephone switch that it wanted to place a call) and signaling within the telephone network (so that information on the called party could be received and translated into action by the switch to make the connection). The switches took the place of the cordboard, and led the way for communication by phone to become transregional, then transcontinental, and finally, global.

Improvements in switch design allowed switches to grow with increased demand through the middle years of the twentieth century. However, customer demand toward the end of the twentieth century for increased call volume and additional features for the call itself led to phasing out of purely electromagnetic switches to purely electronic switches. This started in Philadelphia in the early 1960s with the first ESS switch. This prototype, used as an operating switch for a local area near the center of Philadelphia, set the stage for phasing in of all electronic switches. Perhaps ten years later, the sending or transmission of digital data began. This would lead to changes in the transmission characteristics of the network. Having digital facilities gave additional impetus to consider digital electronic switching for the network.

AT&T, as a regulated entity, had only minimal incentive to invest the amount of capital to change to digital switches ubiquitously in the network. Digital switches, also called stored program switches, were designed in the 1970s, but had a slow implementation into the network. Ubiquity of the digital switch would take until the late 1980s or early 1990s, spurred on by competition after divestiture. AT&T became 99% digital only in 1996. As additional features were added to switches, the software running such switches now resembles modern operating systems which have 4-8 million lines of C or C++ code.

10.3 Circuit-switching Technology

Up to this writing, the technology of the telephone networks has been that of circuit switching. This may change over the next few years, as data transmission becomes the predominant service to b e provided (data represents about 10% of the total telephone traffic in 2001), with the great amount of traffic still analog, or voice-grade transmission. Hybrid switches are likely as the voice-grade/data split nears 50% for each; other technologies are likely when the data traffic grows above the 50% point.

The circuit-switching telephone network comprises many interconnected switches, having different functions in the network. The local switch connects local traffic, but also provides a pathway to interexchange carriers, or long distance providers. The long distance, or toll switches, provide connection of messages over very long distances; such switches also provide for tandem traffic, where message traffic is passed from one switch to another directly without any add-drop multiplexing, for efficiency reasons. It is noteworthy that this interconnected set of switches is interested only in routing the traffic from one place to another; content of these messages is of no concern. This set of switches is thus called a communications network.

10.4 External operation of Circuit-switching

Communication by this technology involves three phases: 1) circuit establishment, 2) information transfer, and 3) circuit disconnect.

Before any communication can begin, an end-to-end circuit must be established. For example, if the network consists of five switches, and we want to connect Node A to Node E, we must enter a point-to-point establishment of circuit from A to E. Assume the network is:

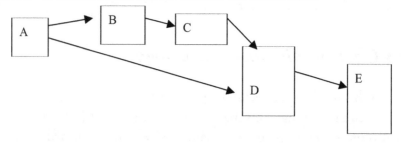

Circuit establishment involves creating an end-to-end circuit in the above figure. For example, Node A sends a request to Node B; the content of this message is an action statement for Node B to establish a circuit from B to E. Should B respond in the affirmative to A, B will then send a request to D to establish the D to E portion of the desired circuit. Should D respond in the affirmative, D will then attempt to complete the circuit establishment by sending a message to E to see if the circuit is complete. If any of the nodes respond in the negative, the sending node must look for other alternatives to route a message to the intended end point. A path must be found in a timely fashion; if this cannot be done, the circuit establishment phase will conclude without success, and the operation will end.

Assuming that circuit establishment concludes successfully, information transfers—the second phase of circuit switching—begins. This phase concludes once all the information has been transmitted. The type of transmission, link procedures, and so on will be set, depending on the features of the network.

Once information in the transfer phase concludes transfer, the circuit disconnect phase commences. This phase amounts to termination of the circuit and making these resources that were in use now available for some other message. This typically involves decommit messages to the other resources.

10.5 Routing in Circuit-switching networks

The process in the circuit establishment phase by which path between the originating node and the terminating node is created is called *the routing*. This process may involve many nodes, or switches, in the network. Certainly, efficiency and flexibility of the network are design factors in any routing process or procedure. Further, the critical factor in the tradeoff of efficiency of the network and its flexibility is the routing (algorithm) strategy. All such routing algorithms will be optimizing one or more of a number of factors. There exist a number of static algorithms (i.e., least-cost route, minimal spanning tree); dynamic algorithms have been added recently. These dynamic strategies make use of current load conditions on the network, which vary, for example, by time of day.

10.6 Signaling in Circuit-switching networks

The commands used in controlling establishment and disestablishment involve signaling in the network. Signaling comprises both the processes of management of messages and management of the general health and operation of the network. The full list of such commands is beyond the scope of this book. However, these commands may be found in the Local Switching System Requirements documentation of Telecordia.

Common-channel signaling

With the traditional signaling, the commands in question are sent via the trunks or connections between switching nodes. This is also called *in-band* or *in-channel* signaling. Here. The same channel or transmission facility is used for both signaling information and data transfer. However, a more recent development, *common-channel signaling*, uses completely separate facilities to transmit user information and to transmit control signaling. Typically, an *overlay network* to carry the control signaling information exists in parallel with the user network. Thus, control signaling can be kept separate in a real way from the user information.

The advantages of common-channel are: 1) simpler set of control signaling commands, 2) delay in establishing a circuit with circuit-switching, and 3) expanded service offerings through a richer set of commands; disadvantages include the additional cost of implementing an overlay network, and the operational/maintenance costs of common-channel.

10.7 Packet-switching

Packet switching was invented in the 1970s, as a response to long distance companies looking for ways to communicate data more efficiently. Interestingly, this concept has been used, with little change from the first such networks, to the most modern services in data communication today. And, as we have seen before, the prime mechanism leading to this concept was the idea of frames in synchronous transmission.

Operation

Instead of paying the time penalty involved in establishment in circuit switching, packet switching embeds information within the packet of information required for routing, addressing, control and other functions. User information is carried with the control information as one block of data, or *packet*. From the point of view of the user data, the stream of user data is broken up into blocks of user data that can be effectively combined with addressing data into the packets that are then sent to their destination. Each individual packet is independent of the others. Each individual packet is then transmitted and acted on by the switch nodes, until the whole set of user information arrives at the destination of the message.

A number of advantages of packet switching include: 1) greater line efficiency, 2) data-rate conversion is inherent in a packed network, 3) nonblocking nature of the architecture, and 4) use of priorities of the individual packets. Disadvantages include: 1) delay in transmission through the network (since the packets must be buffered to get contiguous data), 2) delay in node transit due to different (and potentially longer) routes, 3) increased overhead information, and 4) increased processing.

Routing Approaches

Two approaches are used in routing user information through the network when the user data is longer than the length of one packet: 1) datagram, and 2) virtual-circuit.

Datagram

The idea of the datagram approach is that each packet is independent of all other packets, either of the same pieces of user information or emanating from the same node. The transmitting computer takes one entire message, breaks it into an appropriate number of pieces and readies each piece of data for transmission in its own packet. When the computer builds the message packet, the computer combines the piece of user data with control information containing destination address, sequence number of the piece of user data in the entire user stream of data, and other information. This packet is quite similar to the internal structure of the HDLC frame, discussed previously. This packet is then sent. However, the actual route of this packet is independent of all other packets, and can, depending on traffic conditions, take a very different route to its destination than other packets. Typically, each node transited by this packet must decide on the basis of the destination of the packet which route will be taken to the next stage of the packet's route. All packets in a datagram approach receive identical treatment.

Virtual-Circuit

The idea for virtual-circuit is to emulate the approach in circuit switching where the entire user message transits the identical path from origination to destination. For such packets, additional information is transmitted in the control information over all packets carrying data of one user message. This information is used by the nodes being transited to specify identical routing for all packets, which contain a piece of the user message. Once the user message has been transmitted, the following packets can have different routing.

Benefits/Disadvantages of the approaches

Datagram	Virtual-circuit
Greater line efficiency	No delay in transiting nodes
Perform data conversion	Better for real-time applications
Nonblocking, but additional delay incurred	Blocking occurs for some messages
Priorities can be used	Less overhead reduces capacity requirements

10.8 Interfacing the network with attached devices

Discussion of packet-switched networks should also consider the interface between the network and the devices attached to it. In circuit switching, a transparent communications path can exist between attached devices; it appears that the originating and terminating devices have a direct link. In packet switching, since the originating computer is required to organize, in some sense, the various fields and user data to build a packet for transport, it is implied that there is some cooperation between the network and originating (and terminating) computers, in order to make this work in a seamless fashion. This cooperation, or the embodiment of this cooperation across the provider and vendor community, has been explicitly written down into a set of international standards, namely ITU-T X.25. We will have more to say about standards later; for now, this set of standard information allows providers and vendors to interface o the physical media level, the computer-to-network level and the routing within the network. It is not our objective to deal with the specifics of X.25; for more detail, please see the ITU or other document for this detail. The importance in this context is that issues, inherent with the packet concept, require information to be disseminated within the service provider *and* vendor community for seamless operation. It isn't important to the end user, which method was used to carry the data but it is critical to the providers, and equipment vendors how the handoffs of data between locations work in field operations.

10.9 Optical Switching—the future of switching

One of the emerging technologies for switching is the *optical switch*. This technology represents a fundamental change of the switch fabric infrastructure. Previously, switches were combinations of electromagnetic and electronic components that actually do the switching function, described above in this chapter. The ever-increasing speeds of the transmission structure have been a major driver to get to optical infrastructure into switches. The reason for this is that the number and character of errors in electronic switches dramatically increases above 600-1000 Mbps speeds. Optical switch fabrics work comfortably at these and larger speeds, because the optics doesn't constrain the basic speed whereas the heat from the electronic switches do present problems at such speeds, particularly with the miniaturization of components at this speed.

Design and implementation of optical fabrics is evolving at this writing. Three different designs are in the beginning stages of feasibility in the field. The design and fabrication of optical chips for the switch is interesting: the way in which photons are rerouted at junction points is by microscopic mirrors, gimbaled in two directions. The angle of the mirror is changed by electric current, which is provided in the same substrate of the chip as the mirrors. Microamps are involved in changing the angle of a mirror, although 140 volts seems common. Mirror sizes are in the range of 400-800 microns.

10.10 Summary

The various switching alternatives offer many options for service provision. Some of these will be discussed in the following chapter. Further, the framing issues of digital data will be central to this discussion.

Chapter 11
—Enhanced services

11.1 Introduction

From the material previously covered, basic telecommunication services are quickly derived. For example, HDLC framing allows for the DS-1 or T-1 service of 1.544 Mbps to be developed, using the framing approach of HDLC for synchronous transmission, the multiplexing ideas of combining 24 voice-grade lines into a single path and the media concepts. The signaling ideas are also used for the basic services. However, with the advent of digital telecommunications, competitors, rather competing service providers, have had additional incentive in deriving services and capabilities in addition to the basic service: additional revenue streams. The Regional Bell Operating Companies, with t he technical assistance of Telecordia, has derived additional switching features on local switches that have become almost ubiquitous by 2000: call waiting, call forwarding, third party calling and so on. As the post-1996 Act environment continues to change the interaction of companies in pursuing customers, the expectation is that more and more capabilities/service offerings will be invented. Some have already come to fruition, and bear discussion in so far as they indicate how companies attempt to use technology to innovate. Three such services/capabilities are ISDN, SONET (leading to ATM), and DSL.

11.2 Integrated Services Digital Network (ISDN)

ISDN, sometimes known as narrowband ISDN, was invented in the 1980s, resulting from the merger of the telecommunications and computer fields. This merger specifically considers the digitally encoded network and computers, and the desire to communicate data (digital) from one computer to another. To this end, ISDN was designed to allow both voice-grade and digital data to be transmitted *simultaneously* over the same facility. This was the first service offering subsequent to the basic services; as such, ISDN was developed in the international standards arena, populated by many parties with vested interests, rather than by a single firm. By 2000, ISDN, or narrowband ISDN, has been widely deployed in Europe, but penetration in the U.S. market has been slow; in fact, for the local service providers in the U.S. who have invested in ISDN, there has been only marginal interest by the customer base. Further deployment likely has more to do with very high-speed data transfer mechanisms (such as high-speed optical switching and transmission alternatives). That said, ISDN has led the way to enhanced service/capability offerings.

11.3 Overall Objectives of ISDN

At its inception, ISDN was intended to be a new service offering, designed to replace the existing public networks, in order to offer a number of new services. Whereas this gained ground in Europe, the U.S. and the Pacific Rim have not warmed up to widely accepting ISDN. Part of the reason (in addition to the above thought) include service provider pricing to the end user (initially, $150/month), and development of more alternatives with better price/performance. Having been developed in the international standards, the interfaces for ISDN are available for the end user. The overall objectives of ISDN are: 1) support for voice and data applications which use a limited set of standardized interfaces, 2) support for both circuit- and packet-switching, and 3) layered protocol architecture for access.

11.4 Transmission architecture

The digital channel between switch and end user is comprised of a number of communication channels. Specifically, an access link can be comprised of:

1) B-channel: capacity of 64 kbps
2) D-channel: capacity of either 16 or 64 kbps
3) H-channel: one of the following—384, 1536 or 1920 kbps.

The B-channel is the major end user channel, intended for voice and non-voice applications. Four kinds of connections are possible with a B-channel: 1) circuit-switched, 2) packet-switched, 3) frame-mode, and 4) semi-permanent. The H-channel serves the following purposes: 1) carrying signaling information for circuit-switched calls on related B-channels, and 2) packet-switching or telemetry at those times when no signaling information is waiting for transmission. The H-channels provide greater bandwidth for the end user; for example, fast facsimile, video, and multiplexed streams of data.

Access rates: Basic Access rate and Primary Access rate

To date, two transmission structures have been defined and put into use: 1) basic access rate, and 2) primary access rate.

The basic access rate is comprised of two 64kbps B-channels and a 16 kbps D-channel. All B- and D-channels are full duplex. This package of 192 kbps is intended to serve the majority of end users; it is thought that the general package would contain one voice- and one data channel.

The primary access rate is comprised of 23 64kbps B-channels and a 64kbps D channel. This package is clearly meant for end users with high bandwidth needs: businesses and other entities. In Europe, the package is for 30 64kbps B-channels and two 64kbps D-channels. In both Europe and North America, the D-channels are used for signaling.

11.5 Synchronous Optical Network (SONET/SDH)

One of the competing factors in the North American market, the desire for more and more bandwidth for Internet and World Wide Web applications, led to the development of SONET (known as SDH in Europe). Telecordia was an instrumental player in the development of SONET. Originally conceived as a method for add-drop multiplexing, SONET and its use of optical fiber had greater bandwidth and better error properties; the thought arose from these properties that an optical hierarchy of digital transmission could be developed. Many players with strong (and divergent) vested interests came together in the North American standards body (T1X1 of Committee T1) to develop the SONET signal hierarchy, the first four levels of which are:

OC-1	51.84 Mbps of which 50.11Mbps is payload
OC-3	155.52 Mbps of which 150.34Mbps is payload
OC-9	466.56 Mbps of which 451.01Mbps is payload
OC-48	2488.32 Mbps of which 2405.38Mbps is payload

The OC designation represents an optical signal, carried by optical fiber and using optical equipment for switching; an STS equivalent to the OC designation denotes an electrical equivalent used instead of the optical transmission.

The fundamental concept of SONET is its frame structure or format. The SONET frame is a 9 by 90 octet logical structure that is transmitted every 125 microseconds, leading to a data rate of 51.84 Mbps. The remainder of the hierarchy is comprised of triads of the OC-1 structure (3,9,12,18,24,36,48,96,etc.). Along with the payload, there are three types of overhead: 1) section, 2) line, and 3) path. Overhead of the transmission signal from termination to termination of the circuit is called the section overhead; overhead from end of circuit in the line to the other end is line overhead; the overhead of the logical paths that signals make is the path designation.

The following is an illustration of this:

OC-1 frame format

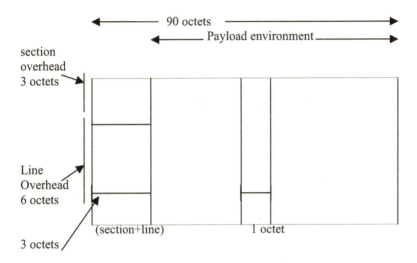

SONET rings

SONET rings is an outgrowth of the SONET frame and hierarchy. In many metropolitan locations, SONET rings serve hospitals and businesses; they also connect military. These rings are set up in a bi-directional way for greater reliability. If one set of fiber is broken, the other ring of fiber (usually transmitting in the opposite direction from the initial piece of fiber) can be used to carry signals on the original ring. This can save switches, which would otherwise have to reroute calls and provide intervening action in other ways to continue the connect.

11.6 Frame Relay and Asynchronous Transfer Mode (ATM)

Frame relay is a network access method that is offered by network providers and shared by many users. This service allows end users to avoid the expense of a private data network, by letting the provider do the work through frame relay service. The advantages of frame relay include: 1) less hardware is required at each location than for a private network, 2) capacity on frame relay is more flexible than on private lines, and 3) frame relay has its own internal backup routes, which eliminate the need for the end user to provide this capability to its private network; its major disadvantage is potential congestion problems.

From an operational perspective, frame relay shares resources among a number of end users. One reason that frame relay networks are faster than traditional packet switching networks is that they do not perform extensive error checking in the network. Should packets be lost or corrupted, it is the end user's responsibility to request resends of such packets and to control this part of the operation. This functional split can be easily justified where network error performance is exceptional; an example is SONET networks, where error performance is three orders of magnitude better than coaxial networks.

Frame relay is an increasingly popular network strategy, particularly when organizations add new applications or build new networks. Time is saved by: 1) avoiding leasing individual private lines, 2) purchasing equipment and designing and 3) maintaining the network.

ATM, or Asynchronous Transfer Mode, is a high-speed switching service with the capacity to carry voice, data, video, and multimedia images. In this sense, providers and end users can carry and use multiple types of traffic over a single physical interface. Information over each connection is organized into fixed-length packets, which are known as *cells*. These logical connections are known as *virtual channels*. We can combine a number of virtual channels into a *virtual path*. Aggregating information into a virtual path has a number of advantages, including increased network performance and reliability.

ATM, like SONET, makes use of a frame format. In ATM, the frame format is comprised of a 5-octet header and a 48-octet payload field. These numbers were heatedly debated in the ATM Forum until agreement was reached on the 53-octet frame. The advantages of a small-size frame include: 1) reduction of queuing delay of a high priority cell, and 2) switching efficiency improvement.

ATM frame

Bit number in octet   8 7 6 5 4 3 2 1

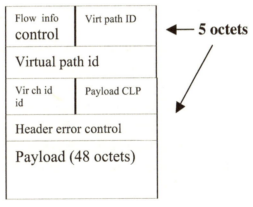

The generic flow control field is used for end-to-end flow control, and is used for the user-to-network interface. If it is the network-to-network interface that we have, this field can be appended to the virtual path ID field. Both virtual path and virtual channel fields are used for routing through the network. The CLP or cell loss priority field is used in cases of congestion within the network.

11.7 Digital Subscriber Line (DSL)

DSL is another network capability, strictly speaking. The purpose of DSL is to enable video and other high-speed data over standard copper cable previously used for voice-grade service. A number of the regional local service providers are offering this service as a high-speed enabler to the Internet and World Wide Web without purchase of completely new equipment by the end user/provider. It also enables telecommuters' access to corporate data and connecting virtual private networks of business.

DSL uses existing copper facilities at the end user premise; however, changes at the local switch in terms of modem and load coil arrangements must be make to accommodate this suite of service offerings. The offerings are made on the basis that no repeaters exist between the local switch termination and the end user termination. The general rule with existing copper medium (i.e., twisted pair) is that end users can be accommodated up to about 15 kilofeet. Should the existing copper have inherent problems, the distance may be much less. If coaxial cable/optical cable already exists, greater distances up to about 20 to 25 kilofeet are possible. It is clear that the offerings depend significantly on the actual medium used, its condition, and the location of the end user relative to the nearest local switch. A number of offerings, having the generic properties of DSL, are as follows:

- ADSL (asymmetric DSL) has an upstream rate of up to 640 kbps, and a Downstream rate of up to 6.1 Mbps.

- HDSL (high-bit rate DSL) up to 6.2 Mbps
- VDSL (very high bit rate DSL) up to 50 Mbps downstream, but requires fiber on.

distances greater than 4500 ft

The Telecom Act of 1996 has been a great aid to faster deployment of a DSL-like service by the RBOCs. Whether this technology will be an effective competitor against the cable industry for high-speed Internet and World Wide Web access remains to be seen.

11.8 Broadband ISDN

The concept of Broadband ISDN (B-ISDN) came about because of the higher-speed alternatives developed concurrently with narrowband ISDN. Today, Broadband ISDN is accomplished with ATM packets. It is interesting to note that ISDN started as a circuit-switched replacement of standard voice-grade telephone service, but is now reinventing itself through the packet switching concepts.

Chapter 12
—Local Area Networks

12.1 Introduction

Local Area Networks, or LANs, represent a special case of networks. The properties of this special case are: 1) these networks are generally owned by the entity which uses the network to connect end user equipment, and 2) the transmission medium for the LAN is shared among the end user devices. In that sense, any device can transmit a message that can be received by any and all devices that are attached to the transmission medium. As opposed to telephone networks, LANs typically are all data networks, and as such, tend to be packet-oriented. As new technology is deployed, the speeds and delivery mechanisms keep changing. The objective of this chapter will be to introduce the fundamental concepts of the LAN, but not to be a complete repository of the many alternatives that exist.

12.2 LAN strategies: organizational evolution

Many organizations have had earlier computer environments, and even earlier LANs that perform data transmission within the firm. Typically, firms have a number of environments, at one time—standalone-, that require interconnection because of changes of the business in question. For example, a firm may have personal computer local networks deployed across a firm, backend networks connecting mainframes, mass storage devices, server farms, and background local networks, each of which has widely varying data transmission needs and distributed location. Combining these disparate subnetworks into a LAN or LANs is usually a lower-cost solution than other alternatives; this solution may also allow the disparate speeds requirements to be met by tailoring pieces of the problem to pieces or individual LANs which can then b e interconnected.

Tiered LANs

The typical computer equipment to be grouped within an organization falls within one of three categories: 1) mainframe, 2) client station, and 3) server machines. In building a LAN to encompass these three, the idea of a tiered LAN, where the mainframes, client stations, and servers comprise separate LANs, connected to a backbone LAN. The idea is that the lower-speed LANs (generally those with the clients and mainframes, which tend to have less traffic) can be attached to the high-speed backbone LAN which then connects the servers to the mix; in this way, a least-cost solution can lead to a workable design of LANs in the organization.

12.3 LAN technology and standards

The technology of a LAN is broken down into three elements: 1) topology, 2) transmission medium, and 3) medium access control. One additional consideration is the wiring layout used by the LAN. In enterprises that are in the start-up to early maturity part of the technology curve, cable/wire layout is generally based on cost, which translates to linear arrangement of cable/wire. For enterprises further advanced, the issue of concern has changed to **ease** of wiring and **availability** of the cable/wire medium; this is known as star layout.

Topology

There are three main options for the designer: 1) bus (also known as 'tree', 2) ring, and 3) star. The star option is used in buildings, in that it conforms to standard wiring practices in buildings. Bus and ring designs are the more preferred in many newer designs. Bus designs are characterized by requiring all stations to attach to a linear transmission medium, via a 'tap'. Rings are characterized by a set of repeaters, which join point-to-point links in a closed loop, or ring. Whereas the bus is bi-directional, the links comprising the ring are unidirectional. Where the star design is used, it is characterized by the fact that *all* stations are connected to the central node, or star.

Choice of an option depends on the following factors: reliability, expendability, performance, scalability and others. Sometimes, the physical limitations of the location where the LAN is to be placed also determine the topology.

Transmission Medium

Many options for the transmission media exist. For wired situations, options include twisted pair, coaxial cable, optical fiber; wireless is also used for a number of situations. Choice of media options depends, like topology, on a number of factors: environment, data type supported, reliability, and capacity are a few.

Impact of standards

The key to the LAN markets is the availability of a low-cost interface, i.e.; the cost to connect equipment to a LAN must be much less than the cost of the equipment alone. What this has done to the market is to create quite high barriers to entry—the vendor community would only support development of a product if a high-volume of production of units could be achieved. This key has led to development of product designs within the *standards* community, supported by both vendor and service provider segments. The standards community in question for LANs is the IEEE 802 committee. Although these standards were originally issued and adopted (in 1985 and later) as U.S. standards, these documents have subsequently been revised and reissued as international standards by the ISO as ISO 8802 standards.

The standards have a number of breakdowns, each applying to a particular option for a LAN. The first standard, 802.2, describes the service features (called the logical link control (LLC)) of the LAN. The next set of 802 details the medium access control (MAC); the MAC layer has four categories:

1) bus/tree/star topologies

2) ring topologies

3) dual bus topologies

4) Wireless topology.

Within the bus/tree/star topologies, two different access control mechanisms give rise to two different suboptions: CSMA/CD and token bus. Within the ring topologies, one option exists—token ring, but a number of physical medium options exist. Wireless and dual bus have one option each. We add some additional detail on LCC, MAC, and the CSMA/CD and token rings.

Logical Link Control (LCC)

This standard describes the services across all LAN topologies. There are three alternative service offerings:

1 *unacknowledged connectionless service.* As mentioned earlier with the datagram operation of packet switches, this operation is simple, without any flow- or error-control mechanisms.

2 *acknowledged connectionless service.* Provides acknowledgement of datagrams

3 *connection-oriented service.* (similar to HDLC with flow- and error control)

Medium Access Control (MAC)

What Medium Access control provides is a mechanism, which provides control in regulating message flow across the set of computers attached to the shared transmission medium. There are two options for such a mechanism: 1) Carrier-Sense, Multiple Access/Collision Detection (CSMA/CD), and 2) token ring.

CSMA/CD (IEEE 802.3 standard)

Historically, this option was the first one developed and implemented in the Ethernet product. This option, from the 'carrier-sense' designation, relies on tones across the physical medium as its medium for transmission of messages. In fact, on voice-grade lines that connect a computer to the Internet, the setup of a connection invariably involves a sequence of various tones, beeps and other sounds (constructed from specific Hertz frequencies), and is directly analogous to this carrier-sense property.

The mechanism for control of access on the medium is an algorithm, based on rules for operation when more than one computer is contending for the ability to transmit (the case for only one computer is trivial). This method is also known as a "contentious" mechanism, for it theoretically allows multiple stations or computers to transmit at once.

The rules for transmission for a station on a CSMA/CD LAN are as follows:

1 If the medium is idle (the carrier-sense property provides the station the ability to

distinguish busy/idle), transmit your message.

2 If the medium is busy (denoted by frequencies occupying the medium), listen on

the medium, until the medium becomes inactive (idle), then transmit

3 If a collision occurs, perform the following:

(Note: A collision occurs when two or more computers on the medium transmit simultaneously. What results is that an interference pattern is created from the two signals, destroying the original information of the transmitting computers. The detection of this interference pattern is called "collision detection".)

4 once a collision is detected, cease transmitting immediately

5 once transmission ceases, wait a random amount of time (the actual wait is computed for a specific station; each station will get a unique wait for the LAN); retry the transmission procedure (i.e., go to Step 1) on the message.

The following illustrates this mechanism:

Msg A Msg B

Time t1

A B

Time t2 (just prior to collision)

Time t3 showing interference pattern

Time t4 (both patterns cease)

Msg A

Time t5 (A is first to transmit)

The advantages of CSMA/CD are: 1) easy to implement, 2) little to go wrong with this mechanism, and 3) inexpensive.

As mentioned earlier, the standards community has built a number of alternatives for the physical medium to work with CSMA/CD. They include: 1) coaxial cable, 2) twisted pair, and 3) optical fiber. Speeds for these alternatives range from 2 Mbps to 100 Mbps in today's implementations.

One consideration for what method is best is to look at the performance. One way we can estimate this is to define a standard length frame. Then we assume an infinite population of users generating new frames according to a Poisson distribution with mean S frames per frame time. If S>1, a collision would result; reasonable throughput results from 0<S<1.

If we include retransmission of old frames, we assume that the probability of k transmission attempts per frame time, for both old and new, is also Poisson with mean G per frame time. Thus, under all loads, the throughput is the offered load, G, times the probability of a transmission being successful, or

S = G times P(0), where P(0) is the probability of no collisions.

We know that the probability that k frames are generated during a given frame time is given by:

$$\text{Pr}(k) = \frac{G^k e^{-G}}{k!} \; ;$$

the probability of zero frames is just . In an interval two frames long, the mean number of frames generated is 2G. The probability of no other traffic being initiated during the entire vulnerable period is given by

$P(0) = e^{-2G}$.

Using S = g times P(0), we have that S = G times e^{-2G}

Finding optimums, we set dS/dG = 0.

This implies that

S = 1/(2e) at G = .5, or

S = .184 or about 18%.

This low utilization has and continues to cause designers to look for other alternatives, particularly if high bandwidth transmission is a requirement.

Token Ring (IEEE 802.5 standard)

Token ring technology had its origins with IBM's LAN product line. This particular strategy is called 'non-contentious', because the mechanism does not allow more than one transmission on the LAN at any one time.

In a token ring, a special bit pattern, called the *token*, circulates around the ring whenever all stations attached to the ring are idle. When a station wants to transmit a message/packet, the station must seize and remove the token from the ring. Once removed, the station with the token can begin to transmit. Once the station is done, it reinserts the token back onto the ring. This algorithm clearly assures transmission by only one station at a time. It should be noted that the reinsertion occurs after the station receives the message/packet it sent and removes the message/packet from the ring.

An implication of the token ring design is that the ring itself must have sufficient delay to contain a complete token to circulate when all stations are idle. Since propagation delay for rings is usually negligible, either a long ring exists, or additional delay may be required to be inserted into short rings. This generally takes place at installation.

The main advantage of token rings is the flexible control it provides; the principal disadvantage is token maintenance, lost or duplicated tokens.

12.4 Bridges

As we have already seen from the tiers concept of LAN design, evolution of virtually all LAN environments expand to more than a single

LAN. In order to link multiple links, as if they were one, the mechanism developed is called the *bridge*. Bridges are devices that are designed to interconnect similar LANs. Such similar interconnection means that the physical layer and Logical Link Control layer (LLC) must be similar. However, it is possible to map a LAN with one Medium Access Control (MAC) layer to another LAN with some other MAC (for example, a bus LAN to a token LAN). The advantages to be gained by the use of bridges include:

1 reliability (if everything is interconnected, failures may spread everywhere; the Bridge limits the failure to one LAN), and Performance (improved performance results from clustering stations where the intranetwork traffic significantly exceeds the internetwork traffic

2 security, and

3 cabling restrictions due to environment or distance.

The design of bridges is particularly important; some of the key issues of bridges include:

1 content or format of the message is unaltered—the analogy is that the message/packet is "copied" across the bridge connection

2 bridges typically contain intranetwork routing and addressing information. Thus, a bridge can correctly address stations on the receiving LAN, even Though the transmitting station has a similar address

3 bridges have no intrinsic limit (i.e., more than two LANs may be connected by multiple bridges).

Chapter 13
—Wireless Networks

13.1 Introduction

Much like the previous chapter, this chapter deals with a specialized subject, wireless networks in this case. With LANs, the shared medium access was the defining issue for network design. Today, the use of a wireless medium for transmission of messages, for both traditional telephone and computer network uses, has grown exponentially, so as to become one of the success stories in involving individuals and business entities, rather than just the business entity, in communicating. As a field, wireless is still evolving, at this writing.

Because of the clear advantages of wireless technology to a business (i.e., no longer tied to a specific geographical location), the growth of various designs has been and remains phenomenal. Analog technologies were developed in the 1980s to provide basic calling and voice mail. Since then, there has been a rush to digital technologies in this market. This rush has partially led to incompatibilities between digital technologies. These incompatibilities remain at this writing, leading to problems when devices with one technology are attempted to be used in a geographical area with different technology, incompatible with the device.

The objective of this chapter will be to discuss the recent history and cover a few of the existing digital services of today.

13.2 History

Prior to the availability of analog wireless technology, users placed telephone calls using "mobile telephones". Both spotty quality and limitations on capacity characterized this radio service. The underlying infrastructure was different portions of the electromagnetic frequency spectrum, which were designated by the FCC for various uses. For example, residential cordless phones are assigned to the 46 and 49 million Hertz (cycle) per second, radio band. Citizens band radio is assigned to the 27, 462 and 467 MHz bands. TV channels2 through 12 and special mobile radio services (i.e., police and fire dispatch) use the 30 MHz to 300 MHz band. As the frequency increases, the radio wavelength becomes shorter. Small wavelengths have greater problems with a number of impairments such as rain and fog. Thus, high-frequency microwave systems are impacted adversely more than the low-frequency systems. Higher-frequency systems cannot be transmitted as far as lower frequencies. (The implication of this is that the newer services, such as PCS, must have transmitting facilities, which are closer together than older cellular systems.

Because of the limited amount of spectrum, the FCC allocates space in order to prevent interference between transmissions. With all these constraints, the goal of wireless has and continues to be one of doing more with fewer facilities. This has led to the hexagonal-shaped "cells" which can be aggregated into the "beehive" arrangement of multiple cells. These cells are constituted such that adjoining cells use different frequencies, but cells that do not adjoin can reuse frequencies.

The second wave of the wireless technology was the change from analog to digital. This shift was done not only for growth, but also for accommodation of advanced services such as caller ID, call forwarding and three-way calling. All digital services use multiplexing in order for customers to share the wireless channels (the more is less idea). However, the European Union chose a standard called "GSM for the digital wireless services; the "GSM" is incompatible with the developments in the U.S. In fact, two different standards of digital wireless services exist in the U.S. They are 1) time division multiple access (TDMA), and 2) code division multiple access (CDMA). These came from two different communities: 1) TDMA from the Telecommunications Industry Association (TIA), consisting primarily of independent telephone companies, and 2) TDMA from an RBOC-dominated body. This situation has led to two types of digital wireless in the U.S.: 1) PCS, and 2) D-AMPS. More on both of these techniques follows. The main features of these services are:

1 both are compatible with either TDMA or CDMA
2 both enable the same telephone features
3 security is good since the multiplexing scrambles the signals
4 spacing of the antennas (or towers) is closer together.

13.3 Digital-Advanced Mobile Phone Service (D-AMPS)

As mentioned above, D-AMPS is a solution to growth. However, this meant breaking the existing cells up into smaller sizes. This tactic adds capacity since each new cell can handle additional simultaneous calls. Further, this leads to more dropped calls and "dead" areas—those areas where problems of overlapping calls into adjacent cells occur. These problems have been a major factor in customer dissatisfaction and have resulted in discontinuance of service.

Other functions needed by customers that are available with D-AMPS include caller ID, call waiting, paging, longer battery life and so on. It should be noted that security/privacy is enhanced with the digital character of D-AMPS, with either multiplexing scheme.

The operational aspects of the signal processors in the handsets enable decoding of the digital bits of the caller ID or paging messages and conversion of these messages into alphanumeric characters. These characters are then displayed on the liquid crystal displays of the handsets.

Providers of cellular service offer both digital cellular service and analog service over the same frequency. Digital service has between three and ten times the capacity of analog. The paging and caller ID are enabled by Signaling System 7, which uses out-of-band, physically separate channels to transmit the information.

13.4 Personal Communications Services (PCS)

PCS was created in order to be rich in features for wireless, but inexpensive. The handsets allow for two-way paging, short messaging service on the LCD, and voice messaging. Along with the conversion and translation of digital bits, the signal processors also code and decode the voice signals from analog to digital at the transmitter and from digital to analog at the receiver. PCS also operates in the 1.8 to 1.9 Gigahertz range, which is not the same as D-AMPS. As from before, the FCC allocates spectrum, and, for PCS, included rules forbidding existing cellular carriers from bidding on frequencies within their own region. The government's goals in this action were 1) to encourage competition among the potential carriers, and 2) to raise money for the U.S. Treasury. These goals have been largely met, evidenced by the drop in all cellular service prices, as well as continued growth in the service itself.

The downside of PCS is its lack of interoperability and its antenna requirements. Since PCS services operate at higher frequencies than D-AMPS, antennas need to be closer together. They are also smaller in height and use less power than D-AMPS. In contrast with standardizing analog methods of providing service, PCS has been deployed with incompatible multiplexing schemes (i.e., TDMA is used by AT&T Wireless, CDMA is used by Sprint PCS). In addition, Europe and other areas are enabled by a still different and inconsistent method of digitizing and carrying calls. Recently, action to partially close the gap between these incompatible methods has been taken, with inconclusive results.

13.5 Internet and Remote Access issues

A need to both transmit and access information remotely from the Internet and corporate databases has led to a number of options for the consumer. The Wireless Application Protocol (WAP) is a protocol for wireless Internet that works across all digital cellular networks. It is menu-driven; the WAP Forum continually maintains the protocol itself. Its ultimate acceptance is still quite uncertain at this writing. Use of the XML (Extended Media Language) in a business-to-business context may also prove interesting in the future.

Chapter 14
—Protocol Architecture (revisited)

14.1 Introduction

The ideas of protocol architecture embody the material that comprises this book up to this chapter. In essence, the client-server model provides the backdrop for a number of the issues covered on what comprises a network. And, even the *term—layers—has* a historical context combining both functions needed for communications and computer science issues of implementing software. What comprises this chapter is the need of "protocol architecture", its implementation in TCP/IP, the relation of TCP/IP to OSI, the impact of standards on these implementations, and the issue of interworking between networks.

14.2 The Need

In the discussion of client-server, and in particular, of message passing, there was mention of the action of sending messages from client to server (or vice versa). What was said was that it occurs as a result of a number of actions; what was glossed over earlier was how each of these individual acts gets done. People like to use analogies to explain a number of events in terms that they feel comfortable using. And, it isn't surprising that voice communications between people is a tempting model. The problem is that the voice model doesn't give an accurate analogy for the electronic communications addressed here. We really must go back to the beginning and derive the computer network issues from scratch.

Typically, there are a number of paths to and from a particular computer. But, this isn't all there is to communications in a computer network. What follows is an idea of what tasks need consideration.

1) the source system (or, transmitter) must not only enable the specific communications path for the transaction, but also make explicit mention to the network being transited of the destination station to which communication is being sent

2) the transmitting system must have a process by which it can find out if the receiving station is not only active, but also capable of accepting information

3) the "application of the transmitting system or station must be able of knowing that the correct "application" of the receiving station can be enabled and perform its functionality

4) incompatibilities between the transmitter and receiver must be capable of being resolved.

These tasks require a process to be enacted both in transmitter and receiver, not unlike the client-server process. Further, what happened in client-server was that functions having some amount of synergy between them were grouped into sets of functionality; consider that operating system functions were grouped in one set dealing with construction of the fields of the message, and another set of operating system functions (sometimes called the "kernel" of the operating system) had the role of "sending" the message to/from the network, and other functions that dealt with getting the message to the right software in the server. This idea of constructing groups or sets of functions to do a specific piece of functionality of the communication, and using the groups as a unit to enable the entire process of communications is precisely the concept of the protocol architecture.

14.3 The functions of communications

The sets of functions, or "*layers*", of the protocol architecture which enable communications between two computers across a network are, as concluded above, really groups of loosely coupled or logically connected functions. It is clear that the composition of the 'set' of enabling functions will change as different aspects of communication need more or less emphasis in the overall design of the architecture at any one time. Thus, membership of specific functions in one group will change, as the functions are perceived to belong to a different function set elsewhere in the design. Further, the groups of these functions cause different architectures, as different perception lead to different placement of functions, causing a different protocol architecture with a different sense of defining the specific communication. This is the reason that both TCP/IP and OSI are legitimate protocols in their own right; they have different objectives and different approaches in making communication work. We will deal with these specific protocols later.

What might be typical sets of functions that we should consider? Consider distributed communications as involving a minimum of two elements that are connecting in order to discuss a third: computers and network to deal with an application. Here again, we are reminded of the client-server model where the client desires work on a particular application to be done by the server (which also has explicit knowledge of the application). As we recall the transfer of message from client to server, we note that we had to get the form of the message in terms that the network could understand, then we had to worry a bout how to transit the network, then how to get the server to accept the message, and, finally, to get the server to do the specific work requested.

From this very general context, we could construe the general sets of functions for communication to be:

1 process of transiting the network
2 process of computer access to the network
3 process of assuring integrity of communication
4 process of logical connectivity to the application.

The process of transiting the network, or "routing" (sometimes called "routing layer"), is comprised of those functions which deal with the addressing of the message at the transmitter, and how the message is acted upon at each node transited in the network, as the message goes from transmitter to receiver. For example, the functions of constructing the address for the HDLC frame—placing the address in the A field of the frame, finding what the address is and what routing mechanism will be used in routing would potentially reside in the process.

The process of computer access to the network may remind one of some of the work in the earlier chapters. The function of converting analog to digital signals or the digital-to-digital translations, the function of aligning the synchronization between transmitter and receiver, and so on are potential examples of functions comprising this process. The process is concerned about the exchange of data between computer and network.

The flow control and error detection/correction typify functions that could reside in the "integrity" layer. This layer concerns itself with reliable transfer of data. This layer can be implemented in many ways, which attest to the number of protocols that differ in what "reliable transfer" means in their environment. It is noted that reliability of transfer is quite independent of the application, or nature of the application. This also is known as the "transport" layer or process.

Finally, the process of logical connections between applications, or "applications layer", deals with the applications themselves. One useful invention that has use here is the *Service Access Point (SAP)*. This concept arises from the way that the client sends a request to the server, where the message has precise knowledge as to which application and the location of this application within the server. The message, from client-server, needs two, rather than one, address 1) the physical (unique) address that allows the client to specify the specific server, and 2) the address of the specific application in the server's memory. This is directly analogous to calling each application by a logical name, so as to keep it separate from all other applications on the server.

As mentioned, the allocation of functions to a particular set has some tie-in with computer science. At the time when protocols were first being discussed, the software methodologies were also being discussed—specifically, modular programming. The idea of modules of software code is applicable here. The sets of functionality, or layers, are simply modules of functions in the programming context. This has been borne out in protocol implementations. For example, TCP/IP has perhaps 300 different implementations worldwide, all of which will work together. These different implementations range from between 6000 and 40,000 lines of C code; clearly, different choices of what and what not to include in the code represents different choices of functionality. Writing these sets of functions in modules makes it easy to add or subtract functions (submodules of code), as different functions are desired.

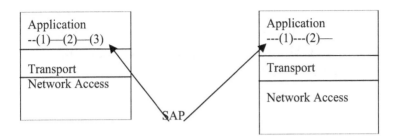

Communications Architecture

14.4 Impact of standards

Given that computers in context of this book are being used for communications, it may be obvious that the mechanisms used at one side of the communication must be the same (or, at least, equivalent) as for all sides. In order to ensure that these mechanisms are the same, the process of standards arose.

For protocol architecture, the underlying mechanisms of the sets of functions and the process of getting to agreement by all concerned is only part of the issue. The establishment of an accepted body by all materially affected and interested parties requires a process itself. We deal with this in the next chapter. Suffice it to say that individuals and individual efforts have developed protocols in the early days of computer communication; this pattern changed when the number of individuals involved in communications grew until a threshold was reached, where having more than a single communications method proved impractical. Once this occurred, setting up an organization to administer the process of designing, formalizing, and adopting the standard became the paradigm chosen by those participating. This has taken a number of forms: international, treaty—based, national industry members, etc.

Two standard protocols exist today. They are 1) Transmission Control Protocol/Internet Protocol (TCP/IP), and 2) Open Systems Interconnection (OSI) protocol. Work on both continues to maintain and expand these products today.

14.5 TCP/IP

TCP/IP represents the protocol that enables communication on both the Internet and the World Wide Web. Historically, Vincent Cerf and Bob Kahn were the key creators of TCP/IP and the two first implementers of TCP/IP products. TCP/IP was and continues to be enhanced and maintained by the Internet Engineering Task Force (IETF); as such, its specifications are accessible on the Internet. These specifications are not standards in the strictest sense: 1) they do not have a formal, rigorous definition agreed to through formal approval procedures by an established body. The internal IETF process for approval is similar to, but not exactly the same as that of a standards body.

From an overall perspective, TCP/IP has been loosely organized into groupings of functions, or layers, as follows:

1 transport layer
2 internet layer
3 network access layer
4 application layer
5 Physical layer.

The application layer and physical layer provide functionality, similar to groupings of functions in all protocols. The *physical layer* deals with groups of functions, which pertain to the characteristics of the transmission medium, signals across such medium and so on. The *application layer* is comprised of those functions enabling the specific work (or, applications of the server) with which the end user has interest. As these two sets of functions are similar across all protocols, we will leave them to discussions in the earlier chapters.

What differentiates TCP/IP from other protocol architectures is the remaining three layers. This differentiation occurs in two ways: 1) the specific actions of the functions within each of the three layers differs from other architectures, and 2) the specific characterization of each layer (i.e., what the purpose of the layer is through this specific set of functions) differs also across other architectures. This is not a value judgement on TCP/IP; we simply note that a different situation would create a different set of objectives, implemented through the architecture. For example, TCP/IP tends to concentrate its integrity and reliability functions in one place, whereas OSI tends to concentrate these functions into two places, because of different objectives.

Within the 'transport layer' (also known as "host-to-host"), the objective is to make the data received to be as identical as possible with the data transmitted. We note that this integrity-reliability issue is independent of the application (not surprising since the designers explicitly had this in mind). Typically, this grouping uses the TCP portion of the protocol. The 'Internet layer' deals with procedures of connecting devices in different networks (or, allowing data to transit different interconnected networks in order to arrive at its intended destination). Two issues arise: 1) the process of routing data across different networks, and 2) the process of exchanging data at the point of interconnection of the different networks. This second issue infers that if the networks at the point of interchange have different protocols, a translation is required in order for the data to transit the second network. The function solving this is that of a *router*, described later in this chapter. Typically, the protocol for this layer is the IP portion. By the way, this situation is not infrequent in the field; it occurs often in the Internet and World Wide Web, and has led to many business ventures, implementing products to solve the issue.

The third grouping of TCP/I is the 'network access layer'. The issue here deals with the interchange of data at the point between the computer (and other end system) and the network to which it is attached. For example, the type of service requested by the end user implies that different software must be invoked in the network to enable a specific service (e.g., circuit switching or packet switching). Also of interest in this layer are the access functions—those doing analog-to-digital conversion, for example.

We note that such functions are relatively independent of the specific network to which the computer is attached.

14.6 TCP Header

For implementations of TCP, information is appended by the transmitting site to application information of the end user for subsequent processing at the receiver site—much like the construction of the HDLC frame. This header field is 160 bits in length, as per the following:

Field name	Bits involved
Source port (or source address)	0-15
Destination port (address)	16-31
Sequence number	32-63
Acknowledgement number	64-95
Header length	96-99
Unused	100-105
Flags	106-112
Window	113-127
Checksum (or CRC)	130-145
Urgent pointer	146-159

14.7 IP Header

For implementation s of IP, a header is also used; in Ipv4 (forth version of IP), the header field was 160 bits, containing a 32-bit field for the source address and another 32 bit field for the destination address. The structure of this 32-bit field defined a hierarchy of network classes within IP. Networks were divided into those with 8-bit network address and 24-bit node address (or station address within the network), those with a 16-bit network address and 16-bit node address, and networks with a 24-bit network address and 8-bit node address. Respectively, such networks were designated Class A, Class B, and Class C. Internet implementations have used this scheme in deriving its addresses: for example, Class A networks are .net, .org, .mil, .com, .edu and so on.

In 1995, due to pressure brought to bear by the exponentially growing address space needs of the Internet and World Wide Web, the IETF decided to expand the address space. This resulted in the address space growing to 128 bits for origination and 128 bits for destination. This new version, Ipv6, is currently being implemented across networks worldwide.

14.8 Operation of TCP/IP Architecture

Operation of this architecture is analogous to the operation of the client-server; one side of the communications becomes the transmitter, readies a message for transmission, 'sends' the message, the method of receiving the message at the receiver, and so on. Let us add detail on the 'sending' of messages here. In TCP/IP, the application layer at the transmitter decides that a communication from its computer to a specific address is desired. Once the application layer completes its functions, control is handed over to the transport layer which then performs its functions. Control is then given to the IP layer and then to the network access layer where the message is enabled for transmission. Typically, a number of networks are transited. At the destination address, the network access layer converts the message to the specific network protocol for this receiver. Then, for further resolution, the IP layer is invoked, then the transport layer and finally the application layer, which can respond to the user request. We note that the SAPs define the specific application to be found on the receiver machine.

We have noted earlier that two levels of addresses are needed. First, the IP layer for routing and other processing in transiting multiple networks needs an address. The second address is needed at the receiver for finding the correct application—it, in effect, is the SAP in the application layer in the receiver machine.

14.9 OSI Architecture

The OSI (Open Systems Interconnection) model, a standard in the international computer and telecommunications standards bodies, is much like TCP/IP in purpose; its difference arises from the very different implementation of the groupings of functions, and, in some cases, the specific functions within the layers.

OSI has seven layers, which are organized as follows:

1 Application
2 Presentation
3 Session
4 Transport
5 Network
6 Data Link
7 Physical.

As with the TCP/IP model, the Application and Physical layers identify groupings of functions beyond the scope of this book, as they deal with the user application and medium issues, respectively.

The Presentation layer deals with providing an independent methodology for various applications in the sense that representations of data can have differences (i.e., EBSIDIC and ASCII have different representations. Abstract Syntax Notation language has been invented to describe such differences.). The Sessions layer provides structure for communications between applications without using the traditional communications structure of this book. Both layers are thus beyond the scope of this book.

The three layers dealing with the communications across a network are 1) Data Link, 2) Network, and 3) Transport.

The Data Link layer provides for the reliable transfer of information across the physical link. This layer also sends frames of user information with additional data, such as synchronization, error control and flow control across the physical link. This layer resembles the Transport layer of the TCP/IP protocol, in that some of the reliability issues of a point-to-point nature are resolved by OSI in the Data Link layer. The Network layer of OSI provides upper layers with independence from the data transmission and switching technologies involving connected networks. The Network layer is responsible for establishing, maintaining and terminating circuits. The routing function (the IP layer of the TCP/IP protocol) is in the Network layer (of OSI). The Transport layer of OSI provides reliable and transparent transfer of data between end points, which can be in different subnetworks. End-to-end error recovery and flow control are provided in Transport. Error recovery and flow control have been enhanced by the OSI design. Also, both logical and physical connections within a service are dealt with in OSI; for example, explicit route control and virtual route control are provided here.

As mentioned, the Session layer provides the control structure for communicating between *applications*. In this sense, establishment, termination and on-going management of active connections between cooperating applications is accomplished. This particular feature is used in the provision of ISDN (narrowband) service. Whereas this feature has been deployed extensively in Europe, penetration into the U.S. market has been limited.

An approximate correspondence between the TCP/IP and OSI architectures is illustrated in the following:

TCP/IP   OSI

TCP/IP	OSI
	Application
Application	Presentation
	Session
Transport	Transport
Internet	Network
Network access	Data Link
Physical	Physical

14.10 Routers and Interworking

In the scheme of things, the capability is needed to transmit across different networks. Typically, we may define something to be a network, such as the Internet, which is actually comprised of many individual networks, connected to each other. The process of using a protocol architecture to connect nodes of different networks for the purpose of exchanging information is known as *interworking*. As one might suspect, there are devices (hardware and software platforms) to perform this work. This device, providing a communications path and needed logic to exchange information between nodes in different subnetworks, is called a *router*.

From above, a bridge is a device involving communications across a single type of network. In order to achieve communications across different networks (interworking), the functions that the router (or routers) require include the following:

- provide a link or route between subnetworks
- provide for routing and delivery of data between applications residing on end systems, which themselves are connected to different subnetworks
- provide the functionality of the above in a way that is independent of the architecture of any of the attached subnetworks.

The last function implies that the router must deal with various issues between the subnetworks, such as

- addressing schemes
- maximum packet sizes
- interface configuration
- reliability.

Chapter 15
—Standards and their impact

15.1 Introduction

The use of standards has become ubiquitous in the telecommunications and/or networking industries worldwide. It seems incongruous that industry would not only accept, but even encourage competitors to sit down and agree on fairly detailed specifications of new networking and telecommunications services and products. Yet, this is what has been happening over the last 5 or 10 years. This chapter has the objectives of clarifying the nature of the standards bodies, their purposes, and the story of success of standards, yet providing providers and manufacturers some differentiation.

15.2 Standards Bodies

Official organizations for the discussion and documentation of technical specifications have been in existence for a long time. These organizations, or 'bodies', have two contexts: 1) part of a national/international treaty organization, where membership is generally by country and voting of approval typically requires a simple majority of countries with a single vote, and 2) an organization administered by a secretariat function (typically, non-voting) and industry consensus that an issue or issues would benefit from discussion in a public forum, where approval depends on the rules intrinsic to the organization. Membership in this industry-sponsored body varies, but generally includes corporations with vested interests in the result of the deliberations, government organizations with ties to the technology and individuals/entities with interests in the topics discussed. All such bodies perform these deliberations along the lines of Roberts' Rules of Order (whereas U.S.-based bodies follow Roberts' rules fairly carefully, international bodies are less strict in conformance).

15.3 The United States Standards bodies

Two standards bodies are discussed here: 1) IEEE, and 2) Committee T1. Both of these bodies have fairly general interests: IEEE with computers and networks; Committee T1 with telecommunications. There are a number of other bodies, which are very focused in a narrow, even single, topic of interest: examples include the SONET Forum and the ATM Forum. We will not deal with such bodies, as once their main focus is resolved, they may disband or move to a different focus. These bodies are quite important, as they start, create and implement work that, initially, may have little relevance to the major bodies, but may, over time, become part of the major bodies.

IEEE, or the International Electrical and Electronic Engineers, is an U.S.-based organization, primarily dealing with issues not of interest here. It is included because of its LAN standards, among others. Due to its focus, the hardware and software manufacturing communities dominate this body. The IEEE secretariat is located in Piscataway, New Jersey, and deals with requests for documentation worldwide.

Committee T1 is the U/S/ standards body dealing with telecommunications standards. T1 came into existence with the divestiture of AT&T in 1983-1984. It was realized at the time by both government and industry that the situation, where AT&T played the role of sole technical resource to outside firms and standards bodies, was no longer applicable in the post-divestiture era. Today, the main players are the RBOCs, the long-distance service providers, the manufacturers, and other materially affected parties, such as the U.S. Federal Government and the CLECs. Over time, the power has gradually been shifting to the manufacturers, as we will discuss later.

15.4 The international organizations

There are four organizations that we discuss here: 1) IETF, 2) ITU, 3) ISO, and 4) the W3C. There are a number of regionally based organizations outside the U.S. that are important: ETSI, the European Telecommunications body is an example.

The IETF (Internet Engineering Task Force) is the international body or consortium dealing with specifications of the Internet, its protocols, and related issues. The body is comprised primarily of computer manufacturers, but also including some interested third parties. One of the products is the maintenance of TCP/IP. One interesting aspect of this body is that the specifications are all available on the Internet.

The ITU (International Teletraffic Union) is the UN body (i.e., treaty-based), located in Geneva, Switzerland, concerned with developing and maintaining international telecommunications standards. The UN secretariat is involved with the maintenance and distribution of such standards. About 90 countries are actively involved, although discussions and voting are dominated by the European block of countries, the U.S. and Canada.

ISO (International Standards Organization) is the international body considering computer and network-related issues. This body tends to have been dominated by the vendor community: IBM and, H-P are examples.

W3C (World Wide Web consortium) was started in Geneva, but has since moved to the Boston area. This body maintains and enhances the infrastructure for the web. One such product is continued maintenance on http and URL specifications. Agreements, once reached, are available on the web.

15.5 The impact of standards

We had originally mentioned that major network and telecommunications specifications are done in a standards body. The reason for this is the globalization of these industries. It no longer makes sense, if it ever did, for the end user to accommodate more than one way of doing something; it also doesn't make sense for the switching elements to contain various vendors' versions of switch software or protocols for interworking. The ubiquity of the product and/or the resulting globalization make standards—a single standard—a must for implementations, whether service provider or manufacturer are involved.

This phenomena isn't limited to the networking and telecommunications industries. The history of U.S. railroads is illustrative. At the time of the U.S. Civil War, it was quite common for different railroads, particularly those in the U.S. South, to have been a result of mergers with several companies across a number of states, which incorporated different gauges of track across their territory. This limited the scope of use to one gauge of track; what happened when one had to travel over long distances is that, at the juncture of gauge change, unloading and reloading of goods was mandatory. During the 1880s, agreement among the railroads, to adopt one standard gauge of track nationwide, occurred. This one change blew away the previous constraints on limitations of reach. Also, in the late 19th and early 20th centuries, adoption of AC power (rather, a standard for such power) and the standard electric plug of the electrical industry was THE vital step in creating the growth of the consumer appliance industry (to say nothing of the electric power industry). The growth and ubiquity go together in their mutual development. All enabled by standards; and, it wasn't and isn't important to be precise about the exact form of standards; what was (and is) important is the existence of an agreement—standard.

However, the actual pieces of the standard do have impact themselves. The industries that populate the networking and telecommunications marketplace have very different motivations, as contrasted with the railroads and electrical power industries. This stems from the vertical integration of the service provider and manufacturer portions of the railroad and electric power industries, as contrasted with the current telecommunications industry composition, previously vertically integrated up to divestiture of AT&T. When the electric power industry follows the divestiture of AT&T, that being disassembled into service provider and manufacturer firms (under way as this is being written), the motivations of the firms should not be assumed to remain a unity of thought.

It may seem obvious, but the standards in this context, are public domain standards. This is a direct result of the internal process of the standards bodies—bylaws exist which strive for consensus among the affected parties of the standard. This results in a "open" standard. This "openness" property has been and continues to be hotly debated in the computer industry. For example, Microsoft has developed its software products in a proprietary way: its current operating system product, Windows, contains code that is not shared on a free basis with the general user. On the other hand, the Sun Microcomputer Corporation advocates today the renting of software products, over the Web with access to all. These are different business models, one being "open" and the other being "closed". In the telecommunications and networking industries, the "closed" standards were developed first, but the "open" standards have been gaining stature over the last 10 years; this trend is expected to continue.

15.6 The service provider motivation in standards

The service providers, albeit competitors in today's marketplace, have similar vested interests in the technical details of an actual standard. The primary, or (at least) the first, goal of the provider was and is to use standards as a negotiating tool to gain power over the manufacturers (or, at least, over the pricing power of the manufacturer). The logic is that if all manufacturers have to build to the same set of specifications, the only issue left to discuss is price; in effect, the providers saw (and see) standards as a way to achieve commodity pricing, and with it, leverage with the manufacturers to achieve the least-cost solution (from their point-of-view). In addition, some of the interconnection issues of the network and telecommunications industry are analogous to the differing gauge issues of the railroad industry. In order to offer services in an unlimited fashion (i.e., globally), the network-telecommunications interests must work in concert to have "the same gauge" solution; put another way, these interests must have a common understanding as to how bits/messages will be exchanged at the interconnection between different company networks in order for services that span both. As the expansion of providers into ever increasing territories continues, this goal becomes more and more important.

Finally, as standards have evolved over the last ten years (and as providers and manufacturers have learned to understand each other and each other's goals more accurately), providers have seen the manufacturers as a resource—aid in leveraging staff time the provider would need to spend sorting out technical alternatives. The provider's view has become more that my firm can partner with another firm (namely, a manufacturer) so that I, the provider, can save my resource. The recent downsizings and consolidations through mergers in the service provider section of telecommunications have made this motivation particularly appealing, in that seemingly more work can be done by less staff.

15.7 The manufacturer motivation in standards

The manufacturer, on the other hand, has its own set of motivations from its viewpoint. First, its dealings with its customer base, the providers, are paramount. Being seen as a "partner" by a provider or a number of providers is equivalent to good will—being seen as a good citizen by the provider community. This can become difficult if one manufacturer becomes "partner" with multiple providers; the providers can lose trust because of this behavior. Still, starting and maintaining any kind of relationship with the providers is very important, as this is where the customer base exists, for the manufacturer. Further, the manufacturer may have a certain monetary interest in the ensuing outcome: the specific definition of a particular bit or the specific language of a definition. For example, the manufacturer may have performed development in secret on the product, and may want certain functionality to be located in specific bits; the manufacturer may have already implemented a specific design in a silicon chip—in order to gain time in getting to market. Should this design be adopted by the overall community in a standard, the ensuing lead in time to market may translate to big money.

There are also subtler issues that impact a manufacturer, and given that particular differentiation within manufacturers may exist, this existence may reduce or eliminate the commodity pricing that the providers strive for. In the process of developing a standard, it is common that some bits are defined in an unusual way: i.e., " for further study" or "reserved". This definition within a standard is typically done to allow for growth or some expansion/enhancement of functionality that is anticipated by the industry, but the specifics are not determined at the present time. Sometimes, this quasi-definition can be utilized by the manufacturer for its own purposes: to implement a proprietary function—secretly—in this bit in silicon to allow for differentiation, when this manufacturer tries to sell product to the provider. Another motivation is that those who work in the discussion of the specifics of a bit are quickly identified ([particularly by the providers) as a "expert" in this standard. The result is to give these individuals abnormally greater power in lobbying for a particular decision by the overall community. Thus, this "expert" can allow a manufacturer to "get their way" in implementation of a product. By allowing an "expert" to provide advice and guidance to a particular provider or a number of providers, this advice may be impacted by the employer of this "expert", to propose a technical solution that is probably indifferent to provider needs, but can give advantage to the manufacturer.

One thing that needs to be addressed is why don't manufacturers go their own way. The globalization of the overall community effectively means that a particular implementation—one that doesn't line up with a standard—can result in reduced market share. This results from incompatibilities arising between the standard and the unique implementation. Even if this incompatibility doesn't arise immediately, as time goes by, and the service changes for the providers, new changes may be imposed on the standard—this may even prove disastrous for the go-own-way manufacturer if the change impacts bit or bits in the proprietary design. Manufacturers will line up to try to disadvantage the proprietary design.

15.8 Customer/end user motivations in standards

Even end users have their own set of motivations that impact the process of developing global, "open" standards. "Why can't I have it now?" is a question that presses for quick resolution and may pressure corporations to make less than optimal decisions. One such example is the situation in 1999 when Bell Atlantic (now, Verizon) offered DSL to the middle Atlantic community of end users, as a "short-term" fix to bandwidth capacity problems in offering fast Internet/Web services to end users. (This was done because longer-term solutions were not available to Bell Atlantic, ubiquitously across its entire area.) This decision can about because Bell Atlantic had fast Internet implemented in some areas, but not others. As corporations and other end users spanned various areas of Bell Atlantic, the end user wanted ubiquitous capabilities, which just weren't feasible (at least from Bell Atlantic). Pressure mounted to make the short-term fix an offering by Bell Atlantic. It is clear from this that, if a service or product offering is made by a provider, it should be ubiquitous at the start across the entire area to avoid situations like the Bell Atlantic one.

15.9 Summary

It is clear that standards (i.e., "open" standards in the networks and telecommunication arena) have been enabled by the impact of globalization of services. Such services have been made more important than they first seemed. This puts increased pressure to be "first to market".

However, the "first to market" idea may be limited in staying power. Microsoft originally thought that the Internet, a noncommercial network at the time, wasn't important in its set of priorities. Ensuing events reversed Microsoft's thinking to the point that Microsoft has made Internet/Web central to their business model; they have been restructuring their products since with this thought in mind.

Chapter 16
—The Web and its tie
with Client-Server
and Protocol Architecture

16.1 The end user and the Web

The World wide Web is an invention that has experienced unimaginable growth over the late 1990s; most, if not all observers, believe that this growth will continue for the forseeable future, and will impact us as few, if any, inventions have over the history of humankind. Whether or not the "Web" in its current implementation succeeds, there will be a network structure, providing the kind of functionality as the web does today.

This chapter considers the evolving network/telecommunication structure of the Web, and postulates that the basic infrastructure of this structure is already known and exists in the previous material, comprising this book. But, let us start with how the end user perceives the Web.

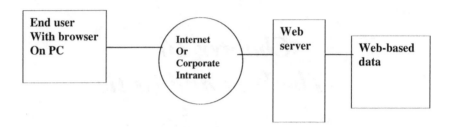

What the above attempts to show are the features of the web that are apparent to the end user. The basic idea of the Web is that pages of information are shared; these pages are "linked", or joined, in some way. The end user has access to the web and these pages of information through a *browser*, which is a software program that is running on the end user's computer system. This browser, from the end user perspective, connects the end user to the Internet (or corporate Intranet) and sends information to the desired Web server, containing the desired pages. The Web server accesses these pages, which are either locally or remotely stored, and requests that these pages be made available to the end user. This results with the requested pages being sent to the end user. Tim Berners-Lee has defined the browser as a web client. We begin to understand the end user perspective as a client-server application where information happens to be in the form of pages (i.e., specially encoded pages). We now take a look at this environment, the Web, from the point-of-view of the detailed components, enabling the work of the end user:

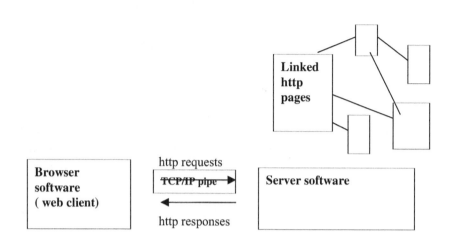

Underlying the physical components, there are some basics about the Web. The pages of the web are composed in the hypertext markup language (HTML). Each page is identified by an address; this address is the URL (Uniform Resource Locator). This address is unique across all pages linked on all servers across the Internet. As an aside, Tim Berners-Lee, in his book—*Weaving the Web*—talks about the efforts to make standard the URL, HTML and http, which we discuss later. The fact that these three issues were made standard is, perhaps, the crucial technical achievement of the Web.

Using the client-server language to talk about how the components of the Web (above) relate, we see that the browser software looks like the operating system functions of RPC (in the client-server paradigm). Such functions form a message, which is to be transmitted to the server. Communication between browser and server occurs in transactions in the form of frames. For the Web, the communications protocol is the TCP/IP protocol; specifically, the routing function of TCP is employed in the transfer of the browser request to the server. Because the end user is interested in getting "pages", or information, which is displayed through the browser through the HTML language, the http (or hypertext transfer protocol) is used to perform the host-to-host integrity function, so that the packets of data, routed by TCP, can be integrated into the page structure. In addition, http instructs the browser to display the page in the display device, using the HTML language. The packets of TCP may use some IP functions, if a message is too big; TCP/IP essentially sends packets which are formed into pages by the http protocol and the page is translated by HTML into the "page" on the display, that we have come to know. Thus, the client-server model is the underlying infrastructure of the web; the protocol issues of separating functionality into different layers for Web communication, is directly analogous to the earlier chapters.

Again, the standardization of the language that the pages would be written in HTML, the unique address so that individual pages can be found (URL), and the protocol glue to take packets that have been communicated through TCP/IP and form pages (through http) is the infrastructure of the web. This doesn't mean that something else couldn't be substituted, should industry agree, for the requisite functions. And, it shouldn't be surprising that groups have been and continue to work on enhanced versions of the web for future implementation. Thus, the understandings of the 'client-server' model and in-depth knowledge of the workings of RPC are important not only for the health and maintenance of the Web, but also for future growth and increased capabilities of the network structure.

Chapter 17—Full circle

The term, "full circle", refers to the closure of the story, argument, or issue under consideration. What we have done in this book is: 1) start with the client-server paradigm, 2) add information about its separate pieces, 3) discuss the various services that are enabled by these functions, 4) discuss protocols from the point of view that such functions comprise pieces of the earlier chapters, and 4) show that an example of a network, the Web, is enabled and enhanced by the various parts of the discussion. The web, or its fulfillment, completes the circle.

That the client-server paradigm is central to networks and telecommunications should not be surprising. The paradigm, at its base, is an attempt to discuss computer communications from the perspective of a third party, looking at the process of how messages are passed back and forth between two processors. In fact, the Remote Procedure Call is seen to be a specific case of the client-server. We have used this RPC to see how the components work and then to build services and products on recombining the components.

The chapters dealing with each individual function—the issues with physical medium, error detection and correction, flow control, routing, and so on—provide the basis for combining these functions into an aggregate. The initial aggregate was the HDLC frame. Parts of that frame relate to individual functions. The concept of protocol is, when we consider each piece of that frame and recombine it, what we really derive is communications (from its disparate parts, and combine them into something that makes sense in the aggregate.).

References

ABRA85   Abramson, N., "Development of the ALOHANET", *IEEE Transactions on Information Theory*, March 1985.

ASH90   Ash, G., "Design and Control of Networks with Dynamic Nonhierarchical Routing", *IEEE Communications Magazine*, October 1990.

BELL90   BELLCORE (Bell Communnications Research , now Telecordia), *Telecommunications Transmission Engineering*, three volumes, 1990.

BERN96   Bernstein, P., "Middleware: A model for Distributed System Services", *Communications of the ACM*, February 1996.

BEYD00   Beyda, W., *Data Communications : From Basics to Broadband*, Prentice-Hall, 2000.

BLAC93   Black, U., *Data Link Protocols*, Prentice-Hall, 1993.

BLAC96   Black, U., *Physical Level Interfaces and Protocols*, IEEE Computer Society Press, 1996.

CASA94   Casavant, T., and Singhal, M., eds. *Distributed Computing Systems*, IEEE Computer Society Press, 1994.

CERF74   Cerf, V., and Kahn, R., " A Protocol for Packet Network Interconnection", *IEEE Transactions on Communications*, May 1974.

COME99   Comer, D., *Computer Networks and Internets, 2nd edition*, Prentice-Hall, 1999.

DEWI93   Dewire, D., *Client/Server Computing*, McGraw-Hill, 1993.

DODD00   Dodd, A., *The Essential Guide to Telecommunications, 2nd edition*, Prentice-Hall, 2000.

EVAN00   Evans, P., and Wurster, T., *Blown to Bits,* Harvard Business School Press, 2000.

FREE94   Freeman, R.., *Telecommunications Transmission Handbook,* Wiley, 1994.

HARB92   Harbison, R., "Frame Relay: Technology for Our Time", *LAN Technology,* December 1992.

HELG91   Helgert, H., *Integrated Services Digital Networks: Architectures, Protocols, and Standards,* Addison-Wesley, 1991.

References (cont.)

HOUS01   Housel, T. and Skopec, E.W., *Global Telecommunications Revolution—The Business Perspective*, McGraw-Hill

JOHN94   Johnson, P., "Domestic and International Open Standards", *Telecommunications Network Mangagement into the 21st Centruy*, Aidarous and Plevyak-editors, IEEE Press, 1994.

KUMA95   Kumar, B., Broadband Communications: A Professional's Guide to ATM, Frame Relay, SMDS, SONET, and B-ISDN, McGraw-Hill, 1995.

MADR94   Madron, T., *Local Area Networks: New Technologies, Emergiing Standards*, Wiley, 1994.

MART90   Martin, J., *Telecommunications and the Computer*, Prentice-Hall, 1990.

MART94   Martin, J., Chapman, K., and Leben, J., *Local Area Networks: Architectures and Implementations*, Prentice-Hall, 1994.

PANK99   Panko, R., *Business Data Communications and Networking*, Prentice-Hall, 1999.

RAPP96   Rappaport, T., *Wireless Communications*, Prentice-Hall, 1996.

RENA96   Renaud, P., *An Introduction to Client/Server Systems*, Wiley, 1996.

STAL95   Stallings, W., *ISDN and Broadband ISDN, with Frame Relay and ATM*, Prentice-Hall,1995.

STAL96   Stallings, W., *SNMP, SNMPv2 and RMON: Practical Network Management*, Addison-Wesley, 1996.

STAL97   Stallings, W., *Local and Metropolitan Area Networks, 5th edition,* Prentice-Hall, 1997

STAL01   Stallings,W., *Business Data Communications, fourth edition,* Prentice-Hall, 2001.

TANE01   Tanenbaum, A., *Computer Netrworks, fourth edition,* Prentice-Hall, 2001.

WHET96   Whetzel, J., "Integrating the World Wide Web and Database Technology", *AT&T Technical Journal,* March/April 1996.

www.ingramcontent.com/pod-product-compliance
Lightning Source LLC
Chambersburg PA
CBHW051243050326
40689CB00007B/1049